A Woman's Soul on Paper

◆

A Woman's Soul
on Paper

◆

Cassandra George Sturges

Writers Club Press
San Jose New York Lincoln Shanghai

A Woman's Soul on Paper

Writers Club Press
an imprint of iUniverse.com, Inc.

For information address:
iUniverse.com, Inc.
5220 S 16th, Ste. 200
Lincoln, NE 68512
www.iuniverse.com

ISBN: 0-595-17143-5

Printed in the United States of America

Dedication

To God, thank you for using my life as a vessel for these words.

To the love of my life, my mother, Mary George. I am who I am because you are who you are. Thank you for your love and support. Momma, I love you so much.

Epigraph

All that I must do is bring my dreams to fruition.
My soul is on a mission
to set my spirit free

No one can define me
No one can confine me

My goal is to be
All that I can be

There are no limitations
the rules are set by me.

Cassandra George Sturges

Contents

Acknowledgements

Thank you, my beautiful children, Sidney and Amanda for your patience and confidence in your mommy, no matter what.

My Aunt Carolyn Harris who has been begging me to write a book since forever.

Dana, thanks for giving me the most wonderful children in the world. I couldn't have picked a better father for my honey buns and best friend.

Michael thanks for respecting my beliefs and dreams even though they aren't your own. Thanks for loving me just the way I am, convincing me of my own worth and never requiring more than my love.

My uncle Fred Harris who gave me my first lessons on love and life. I will never forget.

My sister, Lisa Williams-Banner, thanks for listening to my self doubt at 3 am in the morning and convincing me that I could do it, more times than we have space for in a life time.

Tonia Pitts, Karen Black and Patricia Willis my childhood home-girls who help me keep it real.

Thanks Cedric who would kill a rock over me, and my brother General, who once said, "If you don't like my sister, you don't like me."

Tiheshia Frierson, the greatest assistant in the world. Tih, you are the bomb. Thanks for having my back.

Jeffrey Leonard, my apartment manager. My rent has been late more than on time. Thanks for believing in me. I couldn't have made it without your support.

The Older Man

◆

On the very first date he told me to put my hand under the table while we were eating lunch. I thought this was odd behavior, but it was a public restaurant filled with people, so I obeyed his request. His hand met mine filled with three, crisp hundred dollar bills. I pulled my hand up and was shocked at the money in my palms. " Oh no," I nervously muttered, "I am not that type of girl. I am not a prostitute. I can't accept this money from you." "I am sorry to hear that you think so little of yourself," he said, "because I know that I am not a john. I see that you are a hard-working, single mother and I want to give you some money to take your kids out and buy yourself something nice." He refused to take the money back and told me that I owed him absolutely nothing. I kept his money in a kitchen canister for almost a month, just in case he decided to ask me to have sex with him.

He asked me to attend luncheons and business meetings with him. On several occasions after arriving home he would call and tell me to look in the glove compartment of my car, under my car seat, inside my jacket pocket or the pouch on the side of my purse to find a surprise. He tucked money in these places without me knowing. When I complained, he interrupted me by saying; "I know you would never ask me for anything. Please except this money as a gift. Don't be so prideful young lady, pay your bills." My soul was keeping tabs. How long and how much before he asked me to have sex with him, I wondered.

I felt that I loved him. But sometimes when I look back, I don't know if I loved him or needed him. I have grown to believe that love and need are indistinguishable when the intent is pure. At the time, I had just separated from my husband and could not afford my living expenses. I didn't have the money for daycare for my children while I worked. He told me to find a daycare that I liked and to give him the address and phone number. "Don't worry about why," he demanded when I told him that I couldn't afford it. I felt that I could trust him and followed his instructions. A few days later the daycare called to tell me what time to bring my children in and to inform me that services had been paid for six months. I couldn't believe it! I had never had sex with this wonderful, older gentleman.

He was so good to me that I no longer noticed the all white hair that crowned his head, his huge stomach and the fact that he was old enough to be my grandfather. He was not handsome or physically attractive in the least. I believe it's because he didn't need to be. His wisdom, dignity and generosity could have captured the heart of any woman he wanted. And he knew this. What I loved most about him was that he would make up these wonderful fairytales of unrequited love. In his stories the powerful kings would fall madly in love with the beautiful princesses but due to royal and political obligations he could never have them. There were several times that I doubted his sanity, but not as much as my own for continuing to befriend him. Sometimes I would avoid talking to him because I felt that he was too cheery and too damned happy.

I was working and going to school full-time and barely making ends meet. I wanted him to understand that my husband was gone and that I was hurting, lonely and miserable. He wanted me to understand that I was beautiful and any man who couldn't see this was a fool. I pleaded with him to allow me to drown in my own self-pity and why-me. He forced me to appreciate the amber sunset right in the midst of a sobbing rage. I thought that he was old, and had been harden by life's ups and downs, thus unable to understand the pain that I was feeling. He told me that I was young, ungrateful and unable to see all the blessings that God had given me. I constantly reminded him of all the things I wanted, needed and didn't have. "You need nothing," he would say, " God has given you every everything, beauty, intelligence and determination. The only thing you need is to stop feeling sorry for yourself."

"I need to talk, I am under a lot of pressure with my new clients. I just want to relax, maybe watch television, and order room service. Would you join me at the hotel?" he asked innocently. My heart dropped to the pit of my stomach and sat there heavy and on fire. I had been waiting for this moment. I knew he wanted to have sex with me. Now I would have the opportunity to rid myself of the guilt of accepting his gifts with nothing to offer in return. "Sure," I said confident without wincing, "What time?" Too old to cry and too young to fully understand the consequences of my behavior, I decided that I would give him his money's worth of my soul.

I bought an expensive peach, frilly, negligee to mask the cheap way that I was feeling. While taking a bath, I remember counting my warm teardrops as they blended into the bath water. I was amazed at the way the tears would separate the white bubbles in the tub and reveal my soft, brown flesh. There was absolutely no turning back, so there was no point in thinking about what was lying ahead of me. As I dressed, careful not to look at myself in the mirror, I wondered if this was what prostitutes felt like before having sex with their first customer. I wasn't aroused or anticipating his touch. I was hoping that it wouldn't take long before my debt would be paid in full. I prayed that he would not want to tongue kiss me or touch my breasts.

On the way to the hotel, I stopped by the store and bought a pint of Southern Comfort. "Will he leave the money on the dresser before or after sex," I pondered. "I am a prostitute. I am a prostitute," I slowly repeated to myself. "Damn. I never thought I would do this. I won't tell if you don't, I told myself in my rearview mirror as I got out of my car." When I arrived at his hotel room, he was sitting on the couch fully dressed watching a football game. He had ordered a fruit tray. "The food here is pretty good, order whatever you like," he said. He looked innocent, but I was prepared to give him what he really wanted. What any man really wants. So, I excused myself to the bathroom, sat on the closed toilet seat, drank two thirds of the Southern Comfort, and put on my negligee. I seductively walked over to where he was sitting on the sofa. I sat on his lap with my legs open around his waist. I kissed him on the forehead and then on his lips.

He didn't respond. He firmly held my shoulders to stop me from kissing him. "Look at you," he moaned. What man in his right mind would not want to make love to you, so beautiful, so sweet, so innocent? He guided my body off his lap onto the seat next to him. Goose bumps covered my skin; I placed my hands over my breasts and began shivering. "Is this what you think I want from you?" he asked. "Do you feel that all you have to offer me is your body in exchange for friendship and good conversation? I know it's hard for you to believe that I love you and enjoy your company unconditionally. I am a old man, it wouldn't be right for me to exploit your youth, your freshness, your faith. I watched my mother raise six kids all by herself. I always wondered why nobody would help my momma; just help my momma for no reason at all. Put your clothes back on, please. You have more than sex to offer any man. I don't deserve your body because I gave you money."

I had just failed at the oldest profession in the world. He didn't want me. Somehow he was able to see past the facade. He looked underneath my big-girl smile; expensive lingerie and alcohol induced confidence and found a frightened young woman. I felt emotionally naked, ashamed and stupid. I left the hotel with much more than I came with. I left the hotel with my dignity. I was worried about paying him, but I never thought about what I owed myself.

I Gave it to Him

◆

I was crazy about him because he smelled like Double mint gum, Brut Cologne and marijuana. He sat behind me in my French class in the ninth grade. He wore a navy sailor coat and baggy pants and was always late to class. In class we were required to ask the person behind us their names speaking in French. My heart melted when I turned to ask him his name. In return he asked me for my phone number. I never learned a single French word, but we French kissed in the back of the classroom when the lights were out while our classmates watched documentary films about France.

I decided to give it to him on a snowy, icy, cold day in January. It was a half-a-day of school that I didn't tell my parents about. I was wearing, forest green, stretch, corduroy Sassoon pants, a v-neck, low-cut blouse with horizontal stripes of gold, eggshell white and forest green. I wore a white puffy, waist length jacket that showed the shape of my butt; and according to my mother, back then, too much lip-gloss. My stomach ached with butterflies, my toes were cold and I could no longer feel my ears as I walked to his house. I never counted being raped as losing my virginity. But sex with him would be my official first time in my diary and I wondered what he would feel like.

I had planned to give it to him because I liked the way he pronounced my name in our French class. And because I thought the way he walked was cool and he had gorgeous brown eyes. I gave it to him on that cold day in January because his warm kisses thawed the tips of my ears and he caressed my breasts with his tongue. "My heart is Yearning for Your Love" by the Gap Band played repeatedly on the stereo in his cramped bedroom. On his twin bed, I gave up my virginity, as he whispered the lyrics of the song to me. We did it several times after that. He never asked me to be his girlfriend and I am not sure if I ever wanted to be. But I gave it to him because I wanted to. Period.

I met him at the corner store of my parent's house. He wobbled on crutches as he called to get my attention. "Hey chocolate," he yelled. "I don't know you," I snapped back. I lied. I had heard rumors in the neighborhood about him. He was the neighborhood, "Fonz" character like in the sitcom "Happy Days." "Come here cutie," he begged. "Girl, you so fine you make a nigga` wantta drink your bathwater and slop the juices up with a biscuit." "Uhhh! Boy, you so nasty." I sassed, moving my neck in a circle. I was flattered that the neighborhood thug was interested in me. "I broke into this lady's house and she came back sooner than I expected. I tried to escape by jumping out of her bedroom window. That's how I broke my leg. I served ninety days in jails. I got out two days ago. What else do you want to know?" he said matter-of-factly.

"Oh," I said, taken by his honesty. "So what about those seven digits?" he asked. "Give me your number, my parents will be mad if you call my house because you sound too old for me." I said. He gave me his number on paper that is used for wrapping marijuana. I discussed it with my best friend who convinced me to call him. She reminded me that he could protect me from other thugs and that he had his own car. Convinced, I called him. He talked slow and deep over the phone. He would say "hey girl" without pronouncing the "h" in hey. Sexy. Masculine. Bad boy. I was starting to like him. He took me for long rides in his car. I always wondered why he started the engine by rubbing two wires together under the steering wheel. But, I never asked, too afraid to hear the answer.

While teaching me to drive one day at Belle Isle Park, I decided to give it to him. I accidentally hit another car, and he told the other driver that he was a family man and he didn't want to hurt him. The angry driver threatened to call the police. "Man, shut up! he yelled to the driver. "I just got out of jail. I don't want to go back. But if you keep talking, you leave me no choice." I was too young to have a driver's license. I caused the accident and he defended me. Wow! He turned me on. I was wearing my leopard print panty and bra set, blue jeans and a white short sleeve blouse tied in the front revealing my belly button. I kissed him on the cheek and he quickly moved his face and caught my lips with his.

He parked the car in a deserted area of the park surrounded by trees and water. The windows were steamy from our heavy panting and breathing. My right foot was pressed against the steamy back window and this is what attracted the police officer to our car. We heard some-one knocking on the car in between moans. The officer told us that we had ten minutes to get dressed and move the car. We couldn't stop laughing. I gave it to him one other time and his sister walked in on us. I never loved him. I gave it to him because he appeared tough to the world, but he was tender to me in his own bad-boy way. I gave it to him because he was fun.

Everyone loved and respected him. He was the most popular profes-sor at the university. He was known for bringing in millions of dollars in grant money. The walls in his office were filled with plaques, certifi-cates and awards for excellence in teaching, conducting research and mentoring students. He presented as a gracious, kind, wise man. In his spare time he was a pastor of his own church. He was my professor and advisor.

He kept me after class to tell me that I was a breath of fresh air and he waited anxiously for my arrival to class. Not sure how to respond, I thanked him. He called me one night to tell me, "You're not the kind of woman that a man wants to have an affair with. You would cause a man to leave his wife and family. A man couldn't sleep at night with the mere thought of you sleeping with another man. He would want to possess all of you. I think of you often," he said, "God, tells me that I should leave you alone. I just want you to know that you are special to me." I told him that I was married and that I couldn't cheat on my husband. He assured me that he was not asking me to.

"I am not asking you, 'Would you sleep with me,'" he said, while hugging me tightly and staring at my breasts. "I am asking you, 'Could you sleep with me.'" "Do you mean if our lives were different, I asked?" "How ever you want to answer the question," he said. "I don't know," I said as I begun to cry. "You know what you need to do if you want to graduate from this program. Don't you?" he asked. I pretended not to understand because I knew that there was no way in hell that I was going to give it to him. After this incident, he lost my thesis for my second master's degree three times and eventually stopped returning my phone calls. I completed all of my course work and exams for my doctorate degree. The entire department at the university shunned me. I was forced to complete my doctorate degree at another university.

I questioned my femininity and sexuality because of his proposition. I worried that my suit skirts were too short, make-up too heavy and perfume too obvious. I wondered if I was subconsciously attracted to him and the whole incident was really my fault. "Was I leading him on?" I asked myself. "Surely, I have given it away for much less than to obtain a college degree." I cried myself to sleep so many nights wondering why I didn't give it away when it really mattered. I reasoned with myself that no one would have known and I could have finished school sooner. I want to say that I am proud of myself for denying my professor's advances. But sometimes, I can't help but wonder if I made a mistake by not giving it to him, (especially when I am writing a check for my student loan payments.)

In my heart, I know that I didn't give it to him because I felt that I was smart enough and good enough to earn my doctorate degree by studying and working hard. I didn't give it to him because I wasn't attracted to him, he wasn't funny and I didn't like his attitude. But most importantly, I didn't give it to him because it is mine to give away when and if I feel like it for no reason at all.

Angel by My Side

———————— ◆ ————————

I love her because she understands me even when no one else does. I am sure she was there the day I called him over and over again in the cold, pouring rain. She kept telling me to go home, but I insisted on seeing him, being with him. It took me two hours to stir him from his sleep. I cried and banged and banged on his door. He finally let me in. He never called after I told him that I was pregnant. I left a note on his door telling him that I was going to have an abortion. He never wrote back. He never called. I love her because I am sure she was there each night comforting me when I was saturated in sadness and tears.

The cold, noisy river asked me to jump in. It told me that it could wash away all of my problems. I considered its offer. This meant that I wouldn't have to worry about failing grades, waiting for him to call or wondering why there was nothing special about me. Most of all I wouldn't have to worry about having an abortion. I watched the waves wondering how long it would take before I died and how cold the water was. Hypnotized by the river and paralyzed by my own fear, I stood staring. "Baby, ain't you cold?," said a voice from a small-framed, older black woman who appeared from no where. "Come on in here girl, befo' you freeze to death. Yo' momma would spank yo' butt if she knew you were out here in that little jacket trying to be cute," she lectured. She broke my spell with her chatter as I followed her into the arena. I am sure that she was disguised as the old woman who told me to go home.

I don't know what was worst, the abortion or the time in between waiting for it to happen. I hated myself. I hated eating because I felt guilty. I didn't want to nourish the fetus and make it think I was going to keep it. I didn't want it to get comfortable inside of me and feel that its momma loved or wanted it. I was beyond anger; I just didn't care anymore. My mother badgered me about my hygiene and appearance. Just being alive was a struggle.

Unlike other waiting rooms, there was no idle banter about nothing and every thing. With the exception of one young woman crying on her male companion's high school jacket, the atmosphere was quiet and somber. There were black women and white women, middle aged women and young women. We all shared a moment in time that we couldn't talk about. Talking about it would validate our experience, and like myself, I am sure they were anxious to forget that they were ever there. She must have been pretty brave to follow me in there, a room filled with so much misery and pain.

The thick teardrops stuck to my eyeballs prevented me from seeing the small print on the paper that I was required to sign. The nurse explained what it all meant in a professional, chipper tone. "Signing here relieves the clinic of legal accountability by notifying you of the risks involved. If your uterus is lacerated during surgery and it causes hemorrhaging, we would admit you to a hospital to perform a partial hysterectomy in order to save your life. Additionally, infertility, infection and death are complications of this procedure. Although these things are extremely rare and most likely not to happen, we are required by law to inform you. Trust me, Hon', you'll be all right," she said with a big, rehearsed smile. My hands trembled as I imagined myself dying during the abortion, but I signed it anyway.

I refused to ask God to help me kill my unborn child. Since I was going to hell anyway, I decided to abandon Him first. I had gotten myself into this mess, so, I promised myself that no matter how much it hurt I wouldn't cry or pray. Confused, scared and only fifteen, I felt that this was the right thing to do. Like a big girl, I pushed my bottom to the end of the table and placed my legs in the stirrups. I turned down the nurse's offer to hold my hand and gripped the edges of the gurney with all my might. The loud suctioning noise tugged at my uterus and moved my body up and down. After a loud slurping sound, it was over. The bag containing my panties and a feminine pad was handed to me as they quickly prepared the room for the next girl. I could barely stand, hunched over I crept to the recovery room. I am sure she was there to console me, when a stubborn tear slipped past my numb, aching heart and caused me to sob.

For many years I couldn't forgive myself. I couldn't face God, so I stopped praying and even wanting to. Just like a pesky-well-meaning friend, she rekindled my relationship with God during the birth of my daughter, when the doctors told me that they could not find my baby's heartbeat. I hadn't spoken to Him in years and I wasn't sure if His number was still the same, but I pleaded with Him to let my baby live. "I know I don't deserve to ask you for this favor, but God please, please let this baby live." The doctors told me that my baby's lungs had not matured and that she would be born weighing less than 2lbs. They informed me that she would remain in the hospital for four to six weeks while her lungs developed and her chances of survival were excellent.

My daughter was born five and a half weeks early weighing six pounds and three ounces. She had no medical problems and was ready to be released from the hospital before me. I couldn't believe that God still loved me and blessed me with a healthy, beautiful child. I promised to never stop talking to him again no matter what happens in my life. I thanked God for his unconditional love and forgiveness. We have not stopped communicating since.

I don't remember when the nightmares stopped; dreams of a little girl wearing an all white laced dressed, lying in a casket who looked just like me. I don't remember when I stopped torturing and punishing myself. My days were easy because I could focus my mind on other things. She must have lulled me to sleep through my darkest hours because I am not sure how I made it through each night. Thank you my guardian angel for never leaving my side. I could have never made it this far without you.

The Exploitation of the Black Woman's Beauty

◆

Historically, in America, no other woman has been sexually violated, dishonored and exploited like the African American female. The mainstream media has glorified and perpetuated the stereotype of black femininity as being unappealing in comparison to European women. The historical sexual abuse of black women has aimed to alienate feelings of love, sexual stimulation and intimacy from the black woman's carnal physical presence.

During slavery, white men raped black women and deemed them as lacking the ability to extract sexual arousal from male suitors. They ravished the fruits of the black women's body and claimed its contents were bitter. They stroked her rich chocolate covering and denounced its beauty. The dominant European man peered into the black woman's deep brown almond-shaped eyes, tasted the fullness of her lips and stroked the roundness of her hips, yet disclaimed the power of her beauty and the depth of her femininity. How dare they engage in a perfunctory act of sexual attraction, yet say that the black woman is unlovable and lacks sensuality?

European women have been consistently portrayed as the epitome of beauty and femininity in the American society. Her projected image that defines beauty consists of blond hair and blue eyes. Additionally, she is thin, with narrow hips and a keen nose. The drudgery of maintaining her beauty is displayed in every fashion magazine that tells her that she is not beautiful enough until she loses or gain weight, increase the size of her breast, lips or buttocks; shave, douche and dye her hair. Being beautiful is her birth right and civil duty as demanded by the white male elite. Maintaining this image of perfection is even burden upon her soul. The symbol of her socially constructed, superior beauty is used as a political tool to oppress her as an object of perfection that overlooks her beauty from within.

White women must live up to the beauty standards of Marilyn Monroe, fashion models and the women who pose for Playboy. Although she has been promulgated as having the ability to captivate the sexual desires of white and black men alike, she finds it difficult to compete with the changing ideals of what defines beauty. She is continuously forced to examine her femininity. Even though in the past full-lips had been ridiculed as an unattractive feature for black women, the white woman must expand the size of her lips to maintain her image of flawless beauty.

White women have fought to diminish the objectification of their womanhood, stating they are more than sexual ornaments and demanding respect for their feelings and beliefs. On the contrary, black women have been asserting, despite their strength, and underneath their overalls and callused-hands, they are beautiful, soft and sensuous. White women seek acceptance for who they are, while black women want to be adored for what they are.

To be deemed desirous and beautiful is a blessing that most woman seek, even when she denies it to herself. In most societies femininity is associated with physical attractiveness, the ability to ignite feelings of sexual arousal, and to possess ascetic and erotic appeal. The travesty of the exploitation of the beauty of black women is that the white male used the act of sex to annihilate the sensuality of the black woman's femininity He cajoled the black male into believing that white women were much more desirous, while he continued to have sexual relations with the black women.

The beauty of the black woman has been exploited without admiration and respect from the mainstream populace. But what is most important is that the black woman has managed to accept her own sensuality and beauty. Captivating, mesmerizing beauty smolders from within and its essence can never be destroyed, not even by slavery.

Dance with Me

———————— ◆ ————————

"I want one of those things that make your stomach look flat as a board, waist two inches smaller and pushes your breasts up so that they look firm, round and perfect-the ability to breath is optional," I told the store clerk. "When you find it, I want one too," she responded. We laughed together as I explained to her that I had this wonderful, sexy red dress with spaghetti straps that I was wearing to a ball and I needed to look special. The shoe sales person didn't have the exact red color I needed to match the dress in my size, so I purchased a size smaller in a shoe that made my feet not look as big and matched my red dress perfectly. I chanted to myself, "Style before substance, a girl's gotta do, what a girls' gotta do."

Next, I needed to go to the beauty salon. It would only take 12 to14 hours to have my hair styled. After the beautician has finished with my hair, it is usually pulled so tight that I will need to take aspirins to relieve my headache. Speaking of my new elegant hairstyle, let's not forget the crick in my neck from sleeping with my head halfway off the pillow, careful not to misplace a single strand of hair (Next week's grocery money, you know). Finally, anything that requires the use of my hands must be completed before spending two hours in the nail salon. The day has finally arrived for the special event. I take a bubble bath in my most expensive bath products and generously slather on my favorite perfume and lotion that costs more than the entire outfit.

I feel myself transform into a titillating diva as I carefully line my eyes, apply my eye shadow and add the lip-gloss that gives my lips that sexy, irresistible pout. I practice dancing in the mirror to make sure nothing pops out or wiggles. I ask my kids three times how mommy looks, before seeking approval from my-hard-to-please brother who says, "you'll do." My confidence is boosted and now it's time to go. God knows, I am miserable. I have two hours before the too small shoes become unbearable and the tight corset around my waist stops my circulation. But I look good! Now, do you think for one moment, I want to go to the dance floor to do the hustle with a faceless, bunch of women and men? I don't think so!

I am from the old school; I am one of those women who loves for a man to ask her to dance. The men watch me to determine if he is worthy of dancing with the illusion of beauty that I have created. I like to watch him swallow the lump in his throat as he gets the nerve to request my company onto the dance floor in his sharpest attire. His hairline is evenly shaped and he looks and smells good. It doesn't matter how much money he makes or what he does for a living-he is priceless. It doesn't matter if he is tall, short, skinny or big-I don't care what he looks like, unless I am the last one sitting at the table to watch my girl-friends' purses and drinks (a girlfriend's unwritten rule), who are already on the dance floor-I will always say yes. I came to have fun. I appreciate his presence to complete my fantasy, I feel like Cinderella tonight and he is my prince.

I like to feel a man's strong hands around my hips, see the sweat on his brow and smell his cologne rise from his body as we sway to the beat together. It's dark, hazy and the music is loud. I can't clearly understand what he is saying or asking, I just sense his energy and hear the music and it feels wonderful. He doesn't mind if I accidentally turn the wrong way or haven't learned the latest steps while on the dance floor. We are immersed in our own world and until the end of the song, we belong to each other. Each man in his own way and in his own words says, "Baby, you look good, I like the way you move in that dress." It's rarely personal; he's not trying to pick me up. He's just appreciating the moment and I am grateful that he noticed.

No, I haven't learned to hustle, not because I have two left feet, but because it just isn't me. It looks like fun, but when I want to group dance I go to aerobics. I don't need a man to pay my bills or give me money. For the most part, I enjoy my own company and occasionally spending time with my girlfriends. But there are two things that I will always long for a man to do with me: make love and dance. Dancing, one-on-one with a man is the one social activity that makes me feel most like a woman in a sensuous, desirable, sexy way. So, men if you see me sitting alone while the others are on the floor doing the hustle, please ask me to dance, I only have two hours before I turn into a pumpkin.

The Father's Love is Priceless

———————— ◆ ————————

Men should protect themselves during intercourse if they do not wish to have children. This is true. Smart men protect themselves, but most men don't-this is reality. Then whose responsibility is it, when the woman has told the man whom she is intimate with that she wants to have children, and he in turn tells her that he does not wish to have children, but fails to protect himself? Many women argue, that if he truly doesn't want to become a father, he will protect himself knowing how the woman feels. With a man who is emotionally mature this is correct. But the same goes for a woman who is emotionally mature-why would she want to become pregnant by a man who has verbally indicated to her that he does not want children?

We as women must learn to love ourselves and be extremely selective about the men, who we choose to become impregnated by. Yes, we have a choice. What makes a man an excellent lover doesn't necessarily make him a good father. Although irresponsible, men know that even though it feels good to have unprotected sex with us, these are not the same characteristics he seeks in the mother of his child. In the case of an unplanned pregnancy, the woman is devastated when the man assumes that she should get an abortion and the man is angry about the child support payment that will be taken from his pay check. Both parties are at fault, but the woman has the most to loose so therefore, she has the most to gain by looking out for her own best interest and not assuming that the man will eventually accept and support her pregnancy.

Carrying a child is an emotionally and physically draining ordeal that changes not only our bodies, but also our entire lives. While pregnant we are vulnerable and our self-esteem is delicate, why would we want to entrust our unborn child's future and ourselves to a man who is uncommitted? If a man does not love you prior to carrying his child, your being pregnant is more likely to be a turn-off and place a strain on the relationship than increase his commitment to you.

We can force him to pay child support, but we can't make him love the child or us. Child support doesn't pick the child up from daycare, change diapers at 4 am, cuddle the baby during morning feedings or read bedtime stories. The judge can't demand these crucial necessities that will have a much stronger impact on the child's life than a check. Most mothers will tell you that generally child support doesn't cover the basic necessities of having a newborn baby (Unless the father makes a substantial sum of money).

Lamaze with your best friend is not the same as the child's father, massaging your back and feeling your unborn child move inside your belly. Being pregnant can be a wonderful experience when you and the baby's father are eating Chinese food, jumbo fried shrimp and Mocha almond ice cream at 3 am in the morning. If you have the financial resources to care for a child by yourself this is great, but make sure you have a double dose of patience, love and energy for yourself and the child. Women raise children alone everyday, this is nothing new. But most women will tell you, if given a choice they would not be a single parent.

To make a conscious decision to have unprotected sex with a man who we know is not ready for fatherhood will trap us, more than we could ever imagine to man who does not wish to be tied down. As women, we should practice our freedom of choice by choosing someone who is on the same spiritual page as we are to share our bodies and our lives with because the father's love and emotional support during our pregnancy, delivery and afterwards is priceless.

To the Little Girl Inside

———————————— ◆ ————————————

The hardest person I ever had to forgive was the twelve-year-old girl who followed the thirteen-year-old boy behind the church where he brutally raped and verbally abused her. He stole her virginity and she left her dignity and self-respect behind the church with him. It was even more difficult to forgive the enraged teenager who had abortions, skipped school, drank alcoholic beverages and sorely disappointed her parents. I forgave them this morning.

I have spent my entire life punishing them for making bad decisions. Working hard to cover up their mistakes by working three jobs while going to school full-time, hoping that someday, somehow, I could prove that I was worthy of the air that I was breathing. I majored in the social sciences because I felt that I owed society, because I had been such a bad little girl. I wanted to help delinquent teenagers so that I could warn them not to be like me. Prior to being raped, I was an honor student. I always wanted to be a journalist and travel to see the world. Sewing and creating things in general were my hobbies. But after being raped, the only way that I could validate my existence was by helping others.

While walking home from junior high school, in the late spring, Sam* (not his real name) asked me to follow him behind the church to give him a kiss. I told him no several times. He insisted that I was an awful girlfriend and he only wanted one "real" kiss. I continued to tell him no, until he alluded that I was lucky to even have a boyfriend due to my dark complexion. "Okay, just one little kiss," I said. I followed him behind the church, down the street from my parent's home. Behind the church, we kissed. His hands violated the boundaries of our verbal agreement.

I insisted that he stop and began to walk away. He then twisted my arm behind my back shoving me against the church wall. We began to wrestle on the cement ground. He drug me by my feet, scrapping my back on the ground. I asked him why did he want to do this to me. He replied that he hated the gap between my teeth. I told him that I wanted to wait until I was married before having sex. "You're lucky that any boy is interested in you, you're so black and ugly." he said. He became belligerent and began to punch me. There was a basement window surrounded by an oval opening behind the church. Sam* held my head back over the hole placing a jagged glass bottleneck to my throat threatening to kill me. I felt its sharp point pressing against my throat, as I bargained for my life.

I stopped fighting and allowed my soul to drift away from what was happening to my body. He pulled down my favorite khaki shorts and my panties with Monday embroidered on the side. I felt his cold penis enter my precious body without permission. I heard him buckle his pants and run down the alley. My body was aching as I pulled up my clothes. The only thing that I could possibly think about was what excuse I would give my parents for coming home from school late. "I was attacked by two high school girls," I told my parents. "They wanted me to move out of their way as I was walking down the sidewalk, I refused and we began to fight," I explained.

The next day in school, Sam told everyone in our eighth grade class that he had raped me and imitated how I cried and screamed. He told them that I was wearing yellow panties. I denied everything he said with every piece of my soul. "You filthy, despicable liar, how dare you lie, you tried to rape me, but it never got in!" I shouted. I don't know if anyone believed me, but I convinced myself that this was my truth, because I could not survive any other way. I needed to believe that he never penetrated my body.

I never told my parents or my closest friends, or even myself for that matter about the incident behind the church. Upon entering high school, I began to drink Southern Comfort and rarely attended classes. I failed the ninth grade four times until completing my G.E.D. (the equivalence of a high school diploma). Eleven years later, while away at college, I was writing a research paper on marital rape and read an excerpt from a book where a woman described what it felt like to be raped. She described it in such great detail, for the first time since being raped; I remembered that he actually penetrated me. I became furious with God. I cried hysterically in the library demanding that God tell me why He let someone rape me behind a church, of all places. I asked God if He heard me calling Him or was He asleep. "Didn't you hear me calling You?" I shouted repeatedly, as I was assisted to the school's counseling center. I began to see the school psychologist, but we never discussed the rape.

I cried myself to sleep for two months because I was angry with God and myself. Constantly, reprimanding myself for following that boy behind the church. If I had not followed him for a kiss, my life would be different I told myself. God redeemed Himself, when I read a sign in a little shop near Lake Superior that read: God's wounded make His best Soldiers. Upon reading this, a chill embraced my body and I silently wept. I knew this was God's answer to me. These words comforted me and allowed me to continue to survive.

I realized today that I no longer want to survive. I want to live. I didn't wear my normal heavy eye make-up to work yesterday. I opened the drapes in my apartment wide. I want the sun to come in because I have nothing to hide. I have been so deeply ashamed of my past. I was afraid that if people looked at me they would see the pain and guilt that I was trying to camouflage.

I write this for you, sweet little girl inside of me. The little girl inside who has been yearning to be loved and accepted; I am sorry that I ignored you. It is okay, you did nothing wrong. I love you. I am sorry that I denied you to have fun, read fiction, take an aerobic class or participate in any activity that was not "productive." I apologize for not allowing you to write or dream or be frivolous. I embrace you as the most precious and compassionate entity of who I am. We forgive him, Sam, the little boy who was hurting so much that he was only capable of giving what he, himself was feeling.

Coffee for One

———— ◆ ————

I thought my mother was slowly losing her mind when she would constantly talk about her trials in learning how to make the perfect cup of coffee after my dad's death. "The coffee was too strong today," my mother would say, "I should have added more water. I don't know what's wrong with me lately, I use to make good coffee." Months after my fathers' death, she brewed the same amount of coffee as if my father was still alive. She told me that she would tell my father in her mind that the coffee left in the pot was for him. I listened patiently to my mother, never commenting about her "coffee ordeal." But for almost a year, my mother's initial conversation centered around how good or bad the coffee was that day. Now I understand that learning how to make just enough coffee for her was symbolic of my mother's adjustment to learning how to live without my father and becoming emotionally and financially independent.

My parents were together for over 32 years. They called each other "buddy" and every morning they would drink coffee together before going their separate ways to work. Each night, my mother would perfectly set coffee cups on the counter for herself and my father. They both had their favorite coffee cups and my brothers and I knew we weren't ever allowed to drink from them. Growing up, we had the Mr. Coffee, with the alarm and each morning my family would arise to the aroma of coffee brewing. I still remember hearing the clinks of my parent's spoons lightly hitting the saucers as they chattered. They drank coffee together even when they were angry with each other and not speaking. Even though they were not aware of it, they were communicating as they both made slurping noises sipping their coffee. When I think about it, the only past time that I observed my parents sharing and enjoying was drinking coffee in the morning.

My parents shared much more than coffee in the morning, but the intimate details of their marriage my mother would never disclose to me (And trust me, I don't want to know them). However, it never dawned on me that my mother was really trying to tell me how much she missed my father emotionally and financially, until recently I had my own ordeal over, I am embarrassed to say—a cup of coffee.

I have recently become self-employed, and the seemingly biggest trivial dilemma I have is making coffee just for myself in the morning. So far, it is always too strong, too weak, too much or not enough. Recently, I had a temper tantrum because as I was rushing out of the door to my first appointment of the day, as I attempted to pour a cup of coffee in my favorite driving mug; I realized that I had forgotten to turn the coffee pot on. I sat there on my kitchen floor and cried like a two-year-old. As terrible as my coffee is, I still need it to kick-start my day. After pulling myself together, I realized that it wasn't about the coffee at all. It was about feeling so afraid of being on my own socially and economically.

At my previous jobs, coffee was ready when I arrived or I would make it with the pre-packaged baggies that required no measuring for a full pot of coffee. On occasion, someone would bring in bagels or donuts, but routinely over coffee, my coworkers and I would banter about our children, mates and daily tasks before starting our day. I never thought about how the coffee bonded us in the work place. The cost of the coffee never entered my mind. I think as an employee, I took the coffee for granted, along with the health insurance, predictable paydays and having a boss to cushion my mistakes.

Working for myself, I am so scared. In the past when I worked for others, it didn't matter if I did an exceptional job or merely what was required and expected, my pay was typically the same. I have learned while working for myself no matter what job I do, when and if I get paid is optional. The only thing that is dependable is the bills and there is no one else to rely on but myself. I am still learning time and money management and who to trust. And more importantly, the coffee I make in the morning is still horrible.

But if my mother has learned how to adjust to making coffee for her only, after 32 years of marriage, I know I can do it too.

Over the two years since my father's death, my mother has mastered making the perfect cup of coffee. However in the process, she has dyed her salt and pepper hair blond and wears it in a natural short fade. She has redecorated her bedroom from a neutral pale blue to a soft feminine pink with flowers and white lace curtains. When I visit her un-expectantly, I can hear Tina Turner's greatest hits blasting from the window. As I walk in, I see my mother, in her denim overalls dancing across the kitchen floor singing, "*Simply the Best*" careful not to spill the cup of coffee in her hand. I'll say, "Ma, is there anymore coffee left?" And she would say, "If I knew you were coming I would have made more. Momma, sorry but I only made enough coffee for one."

Good Hair Means—Good Life

◆

Good hair means—good life, good income, good looks and good men. Of all the human races, the Negroid or black woman has the most unique texture of hair. The style of a black woman's hair mirrors her soul. Her hair reflects her values, level of income, degree of education, political beliefs, mood, attitude and age range. It even reveals her genetic heritage more than any other ethnic group. Other races, shave, cut and dye their hair, but the more extreme the hairstyle is from the dominant culture, usually means the woman is denouncing her mainstream values and definition of beauty. Unlike, black women—the more elaborate, unique, distinctive and innovative her hairstyle is-the more likely she has accepted her own beauty and sisterhood of African decent.

There is a rich culture tied to the upkeep of black hair that has created a universal bond among black women. The long hours that black women spend in beauty shops do not only sculpt and mold hairstyles; this intimate environment also shapes and cultivates relationships and knowledge. Even as children, the hairstyles of little black girls require patience and creativity. Selecting the hair accessories to match the clothes, working to part the hair perfectly in diametrical quarters, and oiling the hair's scalp is a shared art among black women. Teaching little black girls how to French braid, twist and plait hair is nature's way of forcing black women to share a unique identity. The sizzling hot-iron-pressing-comb and old-fashioned curlers heated on the stove constructed a labor of love and trust among black women.

The hairstyle of black women reflect their intensity of peace or struggle within themselves. Writer, Terri Macmillan, had definitely, scratched the surface of the depth of the significance of the relationship that African American women have with their hair. Stella's braids in the movie, *"How Stella Got her Groove Back,"* shouted, "No one owns me!"-and illustrated economic, social and artistic freedom. In the movie, *"Waiting to Exhale,"* actress Angela Basset, cut her long hair pending a divorce with her husband of 11 years. The drastic change of the hairstyle was symbolic of not only a new life, but also no longer embracing white standards of beauty and social values. There was an underlying theme of dislike, not for the white woman that he left her for, but for what she represents in the American society's view of ideal feminism. Janet Jackson's hair in the movie, *"Poetic Justice"* reflected her inability to move on emotionally with her life after the death of her boyfriend. The beauty shop owner commented on the new-growth in her hair that was symbolic of Jackson's character lack of spiritual and sexual nurturance.

Traditionally, in the African American culture, good hair meant that a black person's hair was similar to that of Europeans in texture; meaning it was long, wavy or straight. Individuals with this type of hair were deemed as being more attractive and socially "better than" their coarse-haired sisters. The meaning of good hair today means good self-esteem and a good sense of self and culture. The black woman's hair is a statement of individuality with an underlying creative energy of unity and sisterhood.

Are You Happy and Don't Even Know It?

In my quest for monetary success, I assumed that I would also find happiness within its realm. Keeping my nose to the grindstone would surely lead to happiness. Frankly, I found it totally unacceptable for me to engage in any behavior that I considered being frivolous or unproductive. Even the time spent with my children was goal oriented and purposeful. "We are going to Play Land and I insist that you have fun, because this is productive quality family-time," I explained. If my children even mildly hinted at not having the fun of their lives, I would begin to feel like a failure. "What do you mean you liked playing in the sand better? This is supposed to be the fun. I planned this. I paid for this. Do you know how much money this cost?" I reminded them.

The end results, the outcome, the bottom line-these are the most important phrases in a capitalistic society. The journey has very little merit if a tightly defined outcome is not achieved. Looking back on my life, I have learned that it is the journey itself that is the most magnificent treasure of life. There is no gold at the end of the rainbow. The beauty of the rainbow, the array of colors that has no particular ending or beginning is what life's all about.

We live in a society that teaches us that everything that we want that is wonderful and glorious is somewhere else. If you want true happiness, peace, joy and unconditional love, you must pay your dues, so that you can earn these things-not is this life-but when you die and if you go to heaven. We earn grades to go to college, go to college to get better jobs, work to obtain money, date to get married, married to have children, and stay married because of the children. This list is endless. I am learning that my children enjoy each moment.

The planned event does not take precedence over the beautiful ducks and their ducklings crossing the street as the waiting drivers watch in awe until each one is safely across the street. The airplane that glides over the expressway as we pass enchants my children. They won't stop talking about the truck driver who smiled and waved back at them while blowing his loud horn. The dandelions they picked at the rest stop are actually the highlight of their day, insisting on keeping them and placing them in the vase on the windowsill.

The constant search for tangible evidence of happiness prevents it from being discovered. Because it cannot be found-it just is. Searching for happiness is like looking for love or beauty. It's right under our noses and it cannot be quantified or measured in a cup. There are no instructions or road maps that tell us how to get there. We're baffled because we think if we cannot validate it monetarily or by the social approval of others it doesn't exist.

As I contemplated on happiness, I realized that I had it all along and didn't even know it, such as:

When I was pregnant with my son, he moved around in my belly and literally awakened my husband and me during the night. Frequently, my husband could feel our unborn son moving against his back as we both lied on our sides facing the same direction. We were happy and didn't even know it.

Each time I spend the night at my mom's house, the scent of the sheets always remind me of when I was a little girl and fills my heart with joy. This feeling makes me feel so warm and safe inside.

The night before my husband and I married, we stopped along the side of the expressway to kiss passionately in the rain and thunder. The wedding and all of its trimmings could not hold a candle to that kiss.

On the way to the library, my best friend, Kim and I use to buy two 20-piece boxes of chicken nuggets and Snapple peach tea while studying for our master's degrees together. At the time, we complained about the thirty page research papers, the complex financial aid procedures and the awful parking conditions at the university. I'll never forget the bookstores that played classical music and served our favorite cafe' mochas we studied and fantasized about graduation. Graduation day came and went, but somehow I only think about the fun we had traveling to that day.

The first time my eyes met both of my children's immediately after they were born were the most remarkable moments in my life. This must be the truest form of love at first sight.

My first office that was extremely small and without windows, my first car that I bought for three hundred dollars where the bumper was held up with chains were also periods in my life when I was happy and didn't know it. Somewhere in the back of my mind, I was always focused on something bigger, better or more money.

You know what? There was only one period in my life when I was aware of my happiness and that was during the last weeks of my father's life. Each morning I would thank God for the breath in my body and for blessing me with such a wonderful father. I was so grateful for each second that my dad was a live. I was aware of my happiness because I knew that there was nothing grander or more precious than each moment of life. In life, death is the only real outcome and therefore I knew happiness was everything in between.

Are you unaware of your happiness? Look around and cultivate the beauty in your life. There is nothing else but this moment. Yesterday is gone for all of eternity and tomorrow never comes; you are always in the present. Life is a wonderful present. Enjoy it.

The Hickey on Her Neck

◆

I ran into a friend that I had not seen for almost six years. We both worked together as computer coaches at a learning center that was located in an underprivileged housing unit in the inner city. Blair, my friend, was a freshman in college and I was married with two babies and working to complete the last year of my master's degree. We immediately clicked. I was like her big sister, but most importantly we were partners. We worked extremely hard in an environment where crap games were played daily at the entrance door to our learning center. The children who attended the center arranged from the ages of five to fourteen. Many of their little souls had experienced pain that most people have only seen in movies. The community was riddled with crime, but the broken homes, cars and bottles strewn about were merely a reflection of the broken dreams found in the eyes of the residents.

Blair and I shared a special friendship. We provided each other with moral support and would talk each other out of quitting our jobs at the center due to stress. One of us would always say to the other on the verge of quitting, "Homey, what would I do without you down here in hell by myself?" Our jobs were part-time and grant funded, the pay was low, but for the most part we loved our work. We had the opportunity to do our homework on the job when we were not busy. We covered for each other in case our supervisor appeared unannounced.

Blair was dating Trenton, a guy; she had been dating since high school. Trenton was away at college. We all knew when he was home from college because Blair would come to work with these huge hickeys on her neck. The other girls and I would tease her about her passion marks that exemplified young love. A year later Blair received a two-thousand-dollar diamond solitaire ring. Trenton worked part-time at a gym while attending college to be an engineer. Given his financial situation, subjectively, her engagement ring was worth a million bucks.

My husband did not buy me a wedding ring, but I always pretended that it was okay. You know, we had two children right away and bills. When we were Blair and Trenton's age, I was away at college and my husband was working full-time. See it wasn't the fact that he did not love me passionately, he had bills to pay. Right? Whenever I would ask him if he loved me, his response would always be, "I am here ain't I?" Maybe he wasn't the type to declare his undying love symbolically in diamond rings or hickeys. He faithfully paid the bills and was home. Yes, he was watching television, but hey!, he was home, what more could a girl ask for.

Blair and I worked together for approximately two years. I left first to work on my doctorate degree and work full-time as a social worker. We eventually lost touch with each other due to hectic life changes and separate schedules.

I saw Blair recently at the gas station while on my way to drop off my theory preliminary exam for my doctorate degree. Blair was wearing jeans and a T-shirt, dressed just the way I remembered her. We hugged and we both shouted, "Hey homey! Blair anxiously showed me pictures of her one-year-old son. She told me that she married Trenton two years ago and that they had a small wedding ceremony at her mother's house. "We bought a three bedroom house in a subdivision, and Trenton works full-time for the phone company. He completed his bachelor's degree and insisted that I quit my job so that I can graduate this semester. We want to have another baby right away so that the children can grow up close together," Blair gleefully exclaimed. I was so happy and excited for her. I couldn't believe that Blair was now able to purchase her own alcoholic beverages, let alone a mother, student, wife and homeowner.

I started to tell her about my academic and career accomplishments, but when I saw the hickey on her neck, my heart sank. I knew that my life was incomplete, and there was nothing I had accomplished that was worth telling her about while staring at the gigantic hickey on her neck. I wanted her to tell me that she had been mugged or had just made passionate love to her lover while Trenton, her husband, was at work; or maybe she was accidentally hurt while roller-blading, or oh yeah,—the baby scratched her on the neck. I teased her about the hickey on her neck and she blushed with the same love she had for him seven years ago admitting, "You know, we are still crazy about each other." I cannot believe, including high school, they have been together for well over ten years, they have purchased a home together, and the most unbelievable of all—they have a one-year-old son—and he is still putting hickeys on her neck.

Her hickey did not symbolize two immature teenagers in love, as my male friend insisted. That hickey meant that he still desired her. It meant that he not only loved her, but also still in love with her. It symbolized that with or without the house or the baby or the degrees, their love was based on teamwork, and that without all of those material things, they had the most important thing in the world—each other.

I tried to turn up the music and sing happily, but I couldn't fake it, and sobbed all the way to drop off my doctorate exam. It wasn't the material things that she had gained, but the love she never lost, that made my heart ache with envy.

I want this free, invisible thing called love that warriors fight about, singers sing about and writers write about. This shared feeling with another human being that comes from the soul, where we both know that when the head is bald, all the hairs are gray, the stomach is fat, and the teeth are missing,—the only thing that is still intact is the only thing that ever mattered in the first place was our love for each other. And oh yeah, I think I'll take a hickey on my neck, too.

Stretch Marks: The Lines of a Beautiful Love Story

◆

After giving birth to my first child, I was devastated at how my body had changed. I was horrified when I looked in the mirror at my once perfect body, with firm pointy breasts, a flat stomach and flawless skin. I couldn't believe that my breasts were now sagging and twice their previous size. My stomach and thighs were covered with stretch marks; and all I could think about was discarding my revealing clothes, and if I ever had sex again, at least the rapist would not be interested in seeing my marred body. I cried uncontrollably, as the nurse assured me that I was only experiencing postpartum depression. After months of adoring my beautiful baby, I realized that those lines told a wonderful story of how my body changed to adapt to the growing life inside. These lines were the opening of a new chapter in my life.

One of the most ironic aspects of having a baby is that although my body had performed the ultimate epitome of womanhood, to develop a fetus and give birth, I never felt more unattractive. Many doctors and nurses describe the emotional changes that women go through after childbirth as postpartum depression. The Oxford Medical Dictionary describes postpartum depression as, "An emotional psychiatric condition that occurs after childbirth. It is characterized by symptoms that range from mild to intense, suicidal depressive psychosis." Given that I have very little medical knowledge, I can't say with one hundred percent certainty, but I believe that postpartum depression is mainly psychological adjustment to a new physical and emotional existence. The nurses insisted that I was experiencing a hormonal imbalance, but I knew why I was depressed. I was sad because life as I knew it would never be the same. Yes, for the most part, being a new mother is a joyous occasion, but many things about my lifestyle would change forever.

The physical changes during and after my pregnancy forced me to look at my body with a totally new perspective. Nature rudely informed me that my breasts were not only for sexual pleasure, especially, when they filled with milk and began to ache. Let's not even begin to think about the vaginal stitches after childbirth (episiotomies). The essence of my feminine body was directly connected with nature—the continuation of life. My body provided the tunnel of which life passes through to the physical world. I realized that for me sex was not just an act of love, affection or mere pleasure; but my body could bring to fruition the essence of two human beings. And although, my husband could walk away from our love, our life and our baby, I could not. My body not only provided the avenue, but the foundation that would provide all of the necessities to sustain the life of our child.

In spite of the fact that I was proud of my body's ability to give birth, after the pregnancy was over, I didn't want any visible signs on my body that indicated that life was once there. For some reason, in the American culture, women brag about not looking like they have ever had a child. However, we accept hickeys (passion marks) to symbolize our passion or love for our mate, and let's be honest-are hickeys really physically attractive? Fraternities and sororities brand their members as a symbol of unity. Soldiers are proud of their battle wounds. Unfortunately, most women want to erase any signs of ever being pregnant and giving birth.

Biologically, the female body was designed to nurture and carry babies. During this process, for many women this means weight gain, possibly stretch marks, sagging breasts, and yes! you guessed it, a big stomach. This is the physical reality for most pregnant women. For many women, these physical characteristics described remain for an unspecified amount of time after the birth of their baby. This portrait of the female is physically unacceptable to the media. Before you begin to disagree with this statement, pick up any paper or magazine for women and count the advertisements on how we can improve our breasts, buttocks, stomach, stretch marks, thighs, etc. Far too many women are encouraged to enhance their physical attributes rather than their minds. For example, although Oprah Winfrey and Hilary Clinton are extremely successful and intelligent women, their physical appearance, hairstyle, make-up, and weight is discussed more in the media than their ideas and thoughts on political issues. A close second favorite topic is a woman's relationship with the man in her life.

I guess you're wondering how stretch marks have anything to do with the media's portrayal of women. Well, before the birth of my first child, unknowingly my perception of my self-worth was based of my physical appearance. I prided myself for being able to wear revealing summer clothes, having a flat stomach, and going bra-less. I was no Cover Girl, but I held my own. Even though I was a college student, other than my parents, most of the appraisal that I received from other people was about my physical appearance. Upon embracing my role as a mother, I remember looking at my beautiful infant thinking, "I can't believe that this precious baby came from inside of me." I then began to understand that the stretch marks on my belly were symbolic of my femininity, strength, and beauty. Now when I read those pretty, wiggly lines they say: "You are beautiful and God has blessed your body as vessel to the journey of life."

The Beautiful Woman in the Mirror

───────◆───────

She didn't know I was looking. And I had never seen her before. I was bewildered by the suppleness of her moist skin and the contrast of the darkness of the areola surrounding the nipples of her full breasts in comparison to the rest of her body. Her tummy bulged with sexiness, I had never seen on any other woman before; and her hips and thighs were round, mature and graceful. I found myself mercifully staring in disbelief. Her eyes were engaging and innocent. And her lips invited me to stay. "Who is she?" I wondered to myself as I studied her reflection in the mirror.

While on a business trip in another state, my soul reveled in its new surrounding. My hotel chamber was exquisitely decorated, room service was exceptional, and the only thing I had forgotten to bring with me—was myself. The self who instinctively knew where all of my body's flaws were hidden and each morning she effortlessly reminded me of each one. Even though I was away from home, she was still there making sure that the children were cared for and the bills were paid. This is the self whom I had always depended on and she had never lied to me.

She never meant to hurt me. The purpose of her criticisms is to chisel me into the image of beauty approved of by society. "When you lose weight—you can buy this dress—you can have that man and I'll even throw in the job you have been dying for," she would sternly, but gently whisper in my ear. I believed her. She helped me find creative ways to put my dreams on hold and quiet my desires. I missed her voice of reason. I needed her advice, because the presence of the beautiful woman in the mirror looked like me, and she didn't look like any other woman I have ever known. If indeed this woman in the mirror was me, then I had no idea of who I was.

Contrary to me, the woman in the mirror was sensuous, bold and confident. Unclad, unadorned and undisguised she was certain of her femininity. The mirror reflected but only her body; no make-up, no earrings, no shoes and no clothing; yet nothing was missing. With nothing she appeared complete, and I envied her. Whereas, my beauty was assembled by garments, accessories and perfumes and without these, I felt bare and unattractive. I was daunted, though aroused by her immodesty and the way she freely exposed herself in front of me. I wanted her to be me. I longed to hear the same music that propelled her to passionately sway as if she believed in herself. I desperately needed to feel what she was feeling and see what she was seeing.

"Who are you?" I boldly insisted as tears streamed down my face. Her silence forced me to listen as I watched my trembling hand wipe the tears from my eyes. I beseeched her to answer my plea for acceptance. "Has anyone ever told you that you have beautiful hands, mystical eyes and a pleasing smile," the reflection murmured to me. Spellbound and mesmerized by her beauty, I let her take my hand on a guided tour of my body. My fingers fumbled as they explored previously forbidden places. Places marred by cellulite, stretch marks and blemishes. Places I was reluctant to ever let anyone see or feel because I was so ashamed and embarrassed by its imperfections. I trusted the beautiful woman in the mirror and I let her take me there. I discovered that my body was radiant, soft and lovely. It was I, as I had never seen me before. I held a mental picture of the beautiful woman in the mirror close to my heart.

Upon returning to town, I was eager to share my experience with the woman in the mirror with the self I had left at home. We were going to start a new, more exciting life together, I promised. I was going to tell

her of our plans to buy new clothes and finally go to the mall for a
makeover. Monday morning I would enroll in the ballet class we
dreamed about. But, when I tried to tell her; she was always too busy,
too weary and too tired to listen.

She couldn't hear me because she longed to see her beauty reflected
through the eyes of others. I was anxious to let her know that she is perfect just the way she is, if only she could see herself through her own
eyes and not the clouded vision constructed by others. I wanted her to
know that her true beauty would never be seen in the eyes of others,
unless it was reflected from within her own soul. Sometimes when the
world is quiet and her mind is free, I still invite her to glimpse the beautiful woman in the mirror.

The Unbeaten Path

◆

The more I know who I am, the more I know who I'm not. The broader my knowledge becomes, the narrower are my actions. The most difficult person I've ever tried to be is myself. There are no road maps, instructions or directions. I am on a journey traveling an unbeaten path. When I wanted to please my parents, peers and community life was so much easier. If I was confused or unhappy with my weight, career, school or life in general, it was simple to ask others what was good for me. This spared me the agony of making mistakes and hurting others.

Now that I have chosen the unbeaten path, my life has become much more complex and difficult. Where there was once a road, now there is none. I feel as if I am walking in a beautiful, yet intricate maze of unexpectancy. Now that I have released the self-constructed by others, I feel naked and all alone. I can no longer fit the old silhouette. I now wear what feels good to my soul. I wear the dress that no one else likes, but they marveled at how good it looks on me. It is not the dress they really like, but the way my spirit dances in joy when I move that enchant them. The song, the food and places my soul yearns to explore are now leading the way.

To tell you the truth, I really don't know where I am going; I only know where I am not willing to stay. Some people see my behavior as irresponsible and erratic. The jobs, the friends, the idle activities and conversations are being swiftly deleted from my life. I want to apologize, but I needed them to help me unravel who I am. Only through experience have I been able to discover this mysterious person who resides inside of my soul.

Now I understand that the love affairs that drifted away, the jobs that I quit and the people who I thought were trying to hurt me weren't bad things at all. We were merely on separate journeys passing each other in a single lifetime. My pain and frustration with their actions indicates to me that I lacked a sense of purpose and self. I needed them to validate my existence and lead the way. But you know what is really funny, now that I am more unsure than ever before in my life, for the first time I know who I am.

Puppy Love

◆

Each morning while two hundred miles away at college, he called to ask me what I was wearing, and I obediently answered. Most of the time he disapproved and I dutifully changed clothes at his request. He questioned my whereabouts and each night over the phone I gave him a detailed report of my day. Friends and family implied that there was something unhealthy about our relationship. However, I accused them of being jealous of the attention and love that my boyfriend was giving me. He was my first love and we dated for 2 1/2 years. Although, we were teenagers, our break-up was extraordinarily painful and included the involvement of legal and mental health professionals.

I saw him for the first time in over 12 years last week and he told me, "I have never stopped loving you. I have looked for your sweetness in every woman I have dated including my soon-to-be ex-wife, since we broke up. Everything I have ever done to you, I paid for it twice over. I have tried to recapture that sick-puppy love feeling that I had when we were together. You made me feel like I was on top of the world. Have you ever loved anyone the way you loved me?"

I was addicted to him because he made up for my shortcomings. A college prep high school graduate, tall, thin, and sincere and wore glasses, he was the only boy in our neighborhood to go away to college. Unlike any of the guys I knew at that time, he played successfully in chess tournaments traveling over the United States. At that point in my life I was truant and failing all of my courses in high school and my biggest pleasure was watching my lipstick print on my Eve light 120 cigarettes and deciding which designer jeans to wear. I couldn't believe that a guy like him would ever be attracted to a girl like me. I quit smoking because he told me that it didn't compliment my lipstick.

Our relationship was filled with passion. We argued obsessively over who loved whom the most over the phone and in person. This was our favorite steamy spat that caused us to make love in places that would shame Hustler Magazine. We held hands even when we were angry with each other, which was quite often. He never stopped telling me how he thought I was more beautiful than any woman he had ever known and that made me love him even more. He broke up with me at least once a week and I would literally walk the streets crying and throwing up. I would travel no matter what time of day or distance to explain to him how I would stop associating with my friends and apologize for other men looking at me.

My biggest ambition was to make him happy, be his wife and have his babies. But I was failing miserably at my goal because no matter what I did to please him it was never enough. At some point, I started to find self-esteem in passing my G.E.D exam as opposed to him telling me that I was beautiful. Enrolling in Henry Ford Community College made me feel that some how it wasn't appropriate to let him dictate what I should wear. The things that I admired about him I started to create in myself and what I thought was love begin to fade away. The on and off again break-ups were interfering with my ability to study and I started to grow tired of the uncertainty of our relationship.

"I love you, pooh," he said over the phone after one of our typical fights. "Pooh died," I sadly responded. Pooh was his pet name for me. "What's wrong with you?" he asked. "Our relationship is over," I said, "I am not Pooh and I don't ever want to be her again. I want to be somebody. I want to do something with my life and I don't feel like our relationship fits who I am becoming." No one ever believed me when I told them that I did not plan to break up with him that day. The words just slipped out of my mouth. I think that if I had contemplated leaving him for just one moment I would have lost my courage. He tried to talk me out of breaking up with him, but I could never find it within my soul to go back to what we had.

To answer his question, no I have never ever loved anyone the way I loved him and I hope to never love like that again in the next two lifetimes. I don't walk the streets crying at 3 am in the mornings anymore, not even after my divorce from the man that I will love until I am lowered into the ground. What he defined as love, I experienced as lack of love for myself. Since our break up well over a decade ago, I still run as fast as I can from any man who remotely reminds me of him. I gave him the power to build me up, and thus the power to destroy me as well. I have healed over the years, but in many ways I am still recovering from our sick, puppy love.

If I am Your Queen...

———————— ◆ ————————

"You know the problem with you black women," my ex-boyfriend angrily shouted to me as he dropped me off to work one morning, "is that you don't know how to be a lady. I tried to carry your panty hose for you but you wouldn't let me. I am trying to treat you like a lady by opening the car door for you but when I get over here, you're already out of the car. I have done everything society has told me to do to be a man. I am well educated; I have a good job; I am provider for my family, but this still isn't enough for you black women. Then when you see a brother dating a white woman, you get pissed off and say he is a sell-out or he has no respect for black women. But let me tell you something, I need a woman to act like a woman for me to feel like a man. It makes me feel good to carry your packages for you no matter how small they are or get out of the car and open the door for you. This is what makes me feel like a real man!"

This was not the first comment of this nature I have heard from a black man, but it is definitely the most powerful. In another similar situation, my boyfriend awakened me as he caressed my body and kissed my face whispering, "You are so beautiful when you are asleep." I woke up, smiled and began to nuzzle my face closer to his kisses, he then said, "But boy oh boy when you wake up you are something to deal with." I questioned him about his comment, as I sat up. "What do you mean?" I said. "I just think you are too opinionated, all you talk about is school, money and owning your own business. Why can't you be like other women? Why can't you just take joy in your femininity and beauty?"

Another male suitor told me literally that I think too much. He said that if he wanted to date a Ph.D. he would have remained with his wife. He went on to say, "When I am with you I am not an attorney, I am not a business man, just a man madly in love with a woman. When I tell you something you don't have to rebut it or come up with some intelligent answer, why can't you just be a woman?"

As much as it hurts, maybe there is some truth in these comments. But I can't be less of a person so that a male can feel more like a man. I can't pretend to be weak when I know that I am strong and I won't play these gender role games. Perhaps there has been a misunderstanding; you thought I needed a man as defined by mainstream society such as a breadwinner, head-of-the-household, you-Tarzan-me-Jane, type of man. Maybe you thought I admired the housewives who brag about how much money their husbands bring home, while they take pleasure in splurging his money on body massages, breasts surgery and liposuction. Maybe you didn't realize that my identity was not shaped by the actions of others but my own accomplishments and standards that I have set for myself.

You tell me that I am your queen, but you can't accept my strength. I came from a heritage of strong black women who were raped as their husbands helplessly looked on or he would have lost his life. I came from a culture of women who gave birth while picking cotton on the fields-and kept on working. My breasts that you so adore are the breasts of many black women who nursed not only her own children, but those of the slave master. I am the woman who worked from sun up to sun down, side by side her man to feed the black family. I am the grand-daughter of a woman who raised seven children all alone washing and cooking for white folks, but was never able to be home on Christmas eve to watch her own children open their gifts. I have the blood running through my veins of the thousands of black women who saw their men lynched, laid-off and over-looked by the dominant culture. I am the black woman who didn't have time to see if her hair was styled just right, to freshen her lipstick or polish her nails because she had mouths to feed and miles to go before she could sleep.

You say that I am your queen, but yet you won't accept my power. Yes, I understand that there were many opportunities that you were not allowed because white society could not accept an educated black man. But please understand that my power is your power, for I gave birth to our children. My accomplishments are your accomplishments because without your encouragement and sweet lips on my aching body, I could not have made it. It was you, who told me that I didn't need to diet to look like the size-six, women on television, when I questioned my own beauty and femininity. It was you who made me feel that my physical assets was the icing on the cake, but it was my strength, character, wisdom, intelligence and integrity that made you honor me as a person.

You say that I am your queen, then please accept my power; please accept my strength. I don't need you to carry my bags when they aren't heavy. I don't need you to get out of the warm car in the snow to open the door for me while I sit and wait. I need you to help me not as a man, but as a person of equal status. I need you to cook dinner when you know I will be working late. I need you to help around the house more without me having to ask you. I need you to listen to me more and be my friend, not just my lover. I am your queen; therefore that makes you, my king. Please take your rightful seat next to mine and do not complain about the responsibilities that come with the throne of being next to a woman like me.

Why Women, Sometimes Prefer Their Ex's

◆

"I wonder if I am sick or crazy," stated Deborah, my co-worker, "but do you ever wish you had stayed with your ex-husband?" What we intended to be a high-five, turned into a sister-moment where we held hands with our eyes bucked and mouths open. The vibe was so strong, we could not speak.

"I have some things going on in my life now," says Deborah, 31, administrative assistant, "and even though my ex-husband is happily remarried, he is the first person to say 'Bay, I get paid on Friday, or I got $50 dollars you can have.' He offers to fix things around the house quicker than the guy I am sleeping with. My boyfriend is acting up now, but when I add up all the good and bad from both relationships, I should have stayed with my ex-husband."

Tonia, 27-year-old, customer service representative and single mother of one child said, "I think it's simply easier to be with your ex especially when you have a child together. I work and go to school full-time and I need somebody reliable to watch my daughter. When you are not sleeping with a man, he is not as committed to your well being. He wants to do the bare minimum because he doesn't want to make it easy for me to be with someone else.

In addition, it's difficult to date and have a social life because I won't expose my daughter to any man I am dating unless we have been together for a while. When I think about my childcare expenses and my peace of mind of not worrying about my daughter's safety, it takes a pretty big man to fit into those shoes. I literally can't afford to date somebody for a tumble in the sack, pizza and a ticket to the show. He has to step up to the plate. If he can't help me so that I don't have to depend on my ex, he is a liability to me accomplishing my goals. Straight up!"

"All men are basically the same, they all have problems," says Karen, a 32-year-old, nurse, "The real question a woman should ask herself is-what am I willing to put up with? If I knew what I know now, I would have stayed with my ex-husband. I hate starting over. Each time I start over I loose things. I tried to change my ex-husband and he wasn't ready to grow up. I should have been more patient with him and invested more time into changing myself. You can't change people, and it's a burden for them to carry the weight of trying to make someone else happy. I was too rigid. I wasn't flexible with my ex-husband at all; it was my way or no way. The most important thing I learned from my divorce is that life isn't black and white and being right isn't everything.

Yeah, I made some good points, but what good is it when you lose sight of the big picture and destroy the entire relationship. It's okay to be right and keep quiet sometimes. My ex-husband has remarried and he is a wonderful husband to his new wife. I think if we had remained together he would have eventually changed anyway, because I knew he always had it in him. We married young and started a family before either one of us had a chance to mature."

Ms. Winfield, 70-year-old, retired housekeeper says, "My first husband was an alcoholic but he drank at home and brought his money home. My second husband was a drunk who hung out in the streets and spent his money in the streets. I wished a many nights I had stayed with my first husband. I see these young women leaving their husbands, making the same mistake that I made when I was young. I would tell any woman if your husband ain't beating you or your children and bringing his money home, try to work it out!"

After further discussion, we all agreed that we would never go back to our previous relationships. We realized that the reason we fantasize about what-could-have-been is merely because we need to be more attentive to our current relationships or seek new ones. And yes, we all admitted that we left for a reason and would not like to go back to the way things were. Most importantly, through sharing we discovered that unless we ourselves change, we would continue to attract the same type of man. We concluded that the real benefit of looking back at our previous relationship inspires us to learn from our mistakes and apply what we have learned to improve our current love lives.

Mommy's My Best Name

———————— ◆ ————————

"Mommy what is your middle name? what is your real name?; what is your play name?", my six year old son asked. Unthinkingly, I answered him each time as I continued to read. He then moved my book aside and looked directly in my eyes and said, Mommy is your best name, right? "Of course," I said, as I tightly hugged and kissed him. This line of questioning from my son was surprising. At such a young age he appeared to be aware of the various roles played by individuals. And if so, I was glad to see that he was able to understand that the madwoman in the mornings and the drill sergeant in the evenings during the week was not really mommy. The full-time professional and student some-times simultaneously shared the same limited time zone with mommy. This was not always a good combination. But most importantly he made me think about motherhood, and what it means to me.

I cannot think of any other role in my life that has been as rewarding, yet challenging as being a mother; and to date it is still my greatest accomplishment. Motherhood has wisely and gently forced me to appreciate my own mother in a way that I don't think I could have done, otherwise. There were so many things that I took for granted without thinking about it. For example, our home was always filled with my favorite cookies, ice cream, lotions, soaps-everything. It was like magic. I merely consumed without working or contributing in anyway and all of my wants and needs were met. I now understand that my mother did all of those wonderful things because she loves me. She went without so that I would not. My mother worked 40 hours a week, but she always cooked full course home made meals. Through out college, she washed my clothes, mailed me a weekly allowance and was never too tired or busy to tell me that she loved me.

The role model of the perfect mother to me is my mother. The first few years of motherhood were extremely difficult for me because I aimed to imitate her. Having two children that are 10 1/2 months a part, a full-time graduate student, and working over 40 hours a week as a social worker contributed to me falling short from my goal. I refused to cook can goods and hamburger helper. On Sundays, I would prepare dinner, wash, and iron my work clothes for the entire week. I wanted my children's shoelaces to be clean and shoes polished at all times, like mine were when I was a toddler. I was exhausted and a grouch. Why couldn't my pot roast taste like my mother's? How the hell does she fry chicken and not leave the batter in the skillet? Why are my white clothes not as white as my mother's? I felt like a failure as a mother. Dragging my children to the library with snacks and activities at ungodly hours while I did research for my research papers was my reality.

One day as I watched my children drink their hot chocolate (They think it's cappuccino like Mommy's) at my favorite book store, I realized that God blessed me with my children and the only way that I could be a good mommy was by accepting myself unconditionally. The criterion for being a good mother is loosely defined. My kids are happy with me and most importantly they know that I love them deeply and intensely. Motherhood has allowed me to appreciate the beauty of simplicity and nature. Sometimes I am overwhelmed with bills, grades and job performance reviews. I would try to convince God that if he would only give me a new car, allow me to hit the lottery for a million dollars or get that perfect job earning six-figures; yes, yes-then I could truly be happy.

Without these material things, my children constantly remind me of how wonderful life really is. They marvel at watching the snow fall and catching it on their tongues. My children remind me to appreciate the simple, beauty of gazing at the moon, long after I had forgotten that it even existed. "Mommy look!, look!, the moon is following us home." They would tell on the way from the library. I am able to find new joy in roller-skating, riding the giant slide and playing catch. My children are teaching me to appreciate the little pleasures in life. Yeah, I never thought about it before, but Mommy is my best name.

Compassion 101

◆

Although her glare was warm and sincere, she made me feel extremely uncomfortable as I sat eating in a fast-food restaurant with my two children. She looked like the lady in church who would pass you a piece of peppermint candy, just when you thought service would never end. "Momma why is that lady smiling at us," my son asked. "I don't know baby, just smile back and finish eating your food. Maybe she thinks she knows us," I told him. I tried to ignore her, but eventually our eyes met and she gently looked away. My kids noticed that my eyes began to swell with tears. I told them that I had bitten into an onion while I excused myself to the ladies room.

Her presence reminded of how hard I have worked and how far I have come in my life. A six-month-old baby at home, three-months pregnant, five classes from my first masters degree and two-months behind on rent was what my existence boiled down to. My greatest fear at that time was hoping that no one would see me using food stamps. I had worked two or three jobs while completing my bachelors at the University of Michigan-Dearborn and I was a second year graduate student at Eastern Michigan University. My master's degree was on hold because I couldn't afford to pay tuition. None-the-less, I was educated and had earned a college degree so that I could provide for my family and myself. I never ever imagined myself needing public assistance. Due to unspeakable financial hardship and two life-threatening pregnancies

I needed help. I had never looked down upon people who were on welfare. But deep in my heart, I felt that it was beneath me.

Once I stopped feeling sorry for myself I started to use the resources that were available to me. There were computer programs for low-income families and I enrolled in the Ser Metro program where I learned how to type and use a computer. Before then I would pay people to type my term papers. I don't peck anymore; I actually type using the standard format that I learned while pregnant with my daughter. Learning how to type kept my mind off of my problems. Each day I challenged myself to be the fastest typist in my class. I practiced after putting my son to sleep each night. I had never used a computer prior to this program either. I received my certificate for completing the DOS and WordPerfect computer program at the local high school.

Mainly because I was embarrassed I never told anyone that I had a college degree. I will never forget two of my classmates who I frequently ate lunch with. One was an ex-prostitute, who lost custody of her 4 children in Alabama. I saw her a few months ago before she died of AIDS. My other lunch buddy had served time for attempted murder. I heard that she was given life in prison for selling illegal drugs and breaking probation. I really liked them. They made me laugh all the time and we shared a common bond-being human and hoping for a better tomorrow. They reminded me of the cool kids in high school who would never give me the time of day. But this time they were sitting in my group and I was one of them. We were all there because we had nowhere else to go. The judge ordered them to enroll in a skill-training program and I needed to do and be something other than a new mother, again-pregnant and on welfare to maintain my sanity.

Thanks to learning how to use a computer while pregnant, my first job was as a part-time computer coach in a low-income housing community. After my daughter was born, I worked there while completing my master's degree. I nursed my daughter in between my school and work schedule. It was a grant-funded position and the pay was low, but while there I learned how to write grants and develop programs. After I completed school I obtained my first professional position as a foster care social worker. Initially, I loved every minute of it. I loved the families and felt at home with the plethora of problems that they were facing. I could communicate with their souls because I had been there in my own personal hell where you feel that no one really cares or understands what you are going through or feeling.

I am so grateful for what seemed to be one of the most difficult and humiliating periods in my life. The colleges that I had attended did not offer courses on compassion, empathy and graciousness 101 and these are the characteristics that are needed when trying to uplift the human spirit. I understand that the universe has It's own way of teaching us what we need to learn to be who we are. Because to be honest, if given a choice, I would have never signed up for these challenging courses.

The lady in the restaurant was my ADC social worker. We are taught as social workers to never identify a previous client so that they may maintain their dignity. The last conversation that I had with my worker was when she begged me to wait until I received my first paycheck before terminating my ADC benefits. I told her that I could make it three weeks before payday because my self-esteem depended on it. Her last words were, "I wish I had more clients like you." As I walked out of the ladies room, she was leaving the restaurant and she winked at me.

Fireflies

———————— ◆ ————————

The way he pronounced my name with his island accent aroused me. His body was sculpted like an African warrior and I swear his buttocks should have been framed and titled one of the natural beauties of the world. He was gorgeous, sweet and warm; and I wanted him all to myself. I didn't know that the twinkle in his eyes was an illusion and I allowed myself to be taken. Over time my attempts to capture him, began to deplete the substance of our relationship. I became disenchanted with him because he would not mold himself to be who or what I wanted him to be. I was blinded by my own desires and his charm lost its sparkle until everything we shared began to flicker away.

I became acquainted with him one cold October day, while giving him a ride home from class. We sat inside my car and listened to the rain beat rhythmically on the roof to Isaac Hayes' "I Stand Accused." He took my hand and looked directly in my eyes and said, "What if I told you that I was in love with you. What would you do?" His presence was toxic for me and I began breathing deeply, unable to answer, unknowingly at the time, his hypothetical question. None-the-less, I followed him inside of his small, dimly lit, untidy apartment and we talked about love, life and God. He was a complete gentleman and he never violated my space or body. I instinctively trusted him.

During our study rendezvous, he often talked about the poverty in his homeland and his four babies by his high school sweet heart. He said that he felt guilty and blessed at the same time for having the opportunity to obtain a doctorate abroad when he should have been laboriously working to put food on the table for his children. Overcome with sadness he talked about the letters from his "girl" back home that were filled with misspelled words and broken English. "I must make my own back stronger before I can carry anyone, you know," he would say with his native accent. I admired his strength and gentleness and wanted to make his life easier my inviting him into my world.

I anticipated his phone calls and homemade afternoon lunches that he prepared for us. He made me laugh and just knowing him made my life richer. Although we had never made love, when we were together we could feel the dense sexual energy between us. As we studied, cheek-to-cheek, our lips would lightly touch and I could feel his warm, minty breath on my face and neck. We shamelessly flirted with fate. He made it clear to me that he was passionately attracted to me, but was not looking for a commitment and did not want to soil our friendship. "I value you so much as a whole person. I would rather have you in my life at any level than not at all, so let's not tempt the gods," he would whisper in my ear.

I found it increasingly difficult to study while wondering what his kisses tasted like and what his body felt like. I wanted all of him. So I prepared myself to re-establish the boundaries and capture him. I knew his weaknesses and I exploited each one by pretending to cover the cleavage that was left for him to see; moving ever so slowly like a jungle cat in my tightest fitting jeans; and tantalizing him with his favorite scent that filled the air each time I moved. I knew my assets and his liabilities and felt him struggle to resist my feminine charms. I led him to my kisses.

We found ourselves unclad and unsure of where our relationship was headed. Right before the defining moment, he kissed my face and was surprised to find it wet with tears. "Is this what you want?" he inquired breathing heavily. I told him that what we were doing did not feel right to me because we were creating an unhealthy relationship without the proper understanding and expectations. I realized at that moment that I had not been true to him because I snared him without his permission. Beguiled by my seemingly innocence, he considered it an unplanned moment and apologized for taking advantage of my trust. I corrected him and told him all the reasons why I wanted him, but knew in my heart that he could never belong to me the way I needed a man. We agreed to remain friends and to never again allow ourselves to socialize in closed quarters.

My children love to catch fireflies and would chase them endlessly in the late summer. They enjoy catching them in jars with holes in the lids and keeping them as pets, even giving them names. My son always cries the next day because the fireflies no longer light up and slowly die. While comforting my son, I told him that sometimes the best way to enjoy and have something in life is by letting it naturally be itself, because when we capture it, it loses the essence of what it is. To truly catch the firefly, you must to let it go freely and it will never fail to light up for you each summer. It has to live in its own world so that you can appreciate its beauty. I learned this lesson from my relationship with my friend because by setting him free, I was able to keep him in my life. Now when I see him on occasion, his light still flickers and I savior it from afar.

Transitional Man

◆

He took me to the next phase of where I needed to be emotionally and spiritually. His patience, warmth and love were the bridges that lead me to my new lifestyle and self-identity. I knew in my heart that what we shared would only be for a little while because I wasn't sure where I was going. I let him come along for the ride and he became lost in my untamed emotions. I wanted to tell him that it wasn't safe to come with me because I wasn't sure where I would get off or even when. But he was confident that he could protect me and he brought along everything he owned, including all of his love, on a journey to nowhere. And I broke his heart.

Transitional man, you came along during a period of my life when my soul was wounded; my children needed a father; the bills needed to be paid and my body longed to be touched. My life was chaotic and I was confused. I brought nothing along but heavy baggage and an empty heart. You met all of my needs without thinking of your own and generously gave me all of you. My body was starved and I was so hungry for attention; I hungrily took in your kisses, your massive chest comforted me and you made love to me as if I was the most beautiful woman in the world. My barren soul sucked in your kindness, drained your passion and marred your faith in love.

I allowed you to love my children, when I knew in my heart that I was only playing house. You looked so good to me taking them to the park, picking them up from daycare and imitating their father. I didn't have to sit in the emergency room alone, miss work for their dentist appointments or fix their bikes by myself on Christmas Eve-because you were there. Your presence delayed my responsibility of having to listen to my children's unanswered questions about their real father, the pending divorce and my own devastation and sadness. You made my life look perfect and I wanted to be okay. I didn't know that I was pretending to be happy.

Everyone said that we were an attractive couple and I tried desperately to love you back. People were telling me that I was using you, that I was on the rebound and that I would break your heart. But I convinced them that this was not true, because what was there not to love about you. They sensed my ambiguity and wondered what spell I had cast upon you and questioned my sanity for not wanting to keep you forever. You told me that you were taken by my smile, but I took you for all you had. I needed you, but I never wanted you. Can you forgive me?

You taught me how to love, how to give back and how to trust again because you unabashedly shared your soul with me. I know you aren't benefiting directly, but now I know how to love a man. Remember when you told me that the key to my home did not open the door to my heart? You made me aware of the many nights that you felt unloved because I was so preoccupied with everything and everyone, barely lifting my head to say hello when you walked in the door after a long day. I just want you to know that I heard you; it's just that my heart wasn't ready to listen.

You played a lead role in who I am today as a woman. And though your stay was short, it was potent with every lesson I needed to learn to be a better lover and mate. The admiration, passion and respect that echoed from your soul each time I looked into your eyes are now a part of my being. I notice the curves in my back, the slant in my eyes and the richness of my skin tone because you pointed it out to me. I no longer hide underneath the sheets because you declared my body a vision of loveliness. You revealed a side of myself to me that I did not know existed and I like her.

Please don't be offended, but I have never regretted parting with you or missed your kisses, not even once. The truth is I am ashamed of who I was with you. I can't bare the thought of embracing this person who hurt you so deeply. You were open and vulnerable, and I preyed on your love and compassion. To replay the joy during this period of my life means that I would be required to relive the pain. I know this is difficult for you to imagine, but the pain that I was experiencing in my heart outweighed the comfort you were offering me. There were many nights after making love you were sound asleep and could not hear my muffled sobs into the pillow. I needed space and clarity, but your love clouded my vision and direction. I couldn't mourn and heal for trying to love you with a bruised heart.

Handsome stranger, thank you for accompanying me on my journey. Thank you for holding my hand and carrying me when I didn't have the strength to make it alone. You were my angel. You built me up and gave me the strength to get back on my feet again. I am forever grateful to you. It took a pretty big man with a tremendous heart to walk in your shoes. Transitional man, I write this for you. You know who you are. I am sorry, thank you.

Daddy Gave me Strong Roots

◆

This is the most difficult piece that I have ever written. My daddy died on November 7, 1997, 37 days before his 86th birthday. He died of congestive heart failure and had been ill for six weeks, in and out of the hospital. The first day that he was taken to the hospital by the ambulance, the doctors informed us that my father's condition was grave and that he could die at any moment. Those were the most heart wrenching words I had ever heard in my life. I had difficulty grasping the reality that my father was actually going to die. I felt as if an essential part of my being was also dying. My heart was hurting and my soul was aching, but I could not feel any anger towards God, because I had been blessed with the greatest daddy in all of heaven.

At the age of 14, Rebecca Thompson gave birth to my daddy, General James George Sr. in Selma, Alabama in 1911. My daddy told me that his grandfather and uncle (two brothers) came to America on a slave ship. His grandmother was a Cherokee Native American. He could not recall their legal names; however, they were known as "Big Daddy and Sugar Momma." His parents never married. My father had only a third grade education, and by the age of 7; he was on his own. Daddy survived by working as a helpmate on a fishing ship. He mopped the deck, cooked and helped with the other chores. He told me that there were many days that he was hungry and many nights that he had nowhere to rest his head. Daddy married his first wife when he was 19-years-old, and they had one daughter, Mary, my older sister.

My father was 54-years-old when he married my mother, Mary George (maiden name Harris), and started a new family raising three children, my two brothers, Cedric, General Jr. and me. When I was born, my daddy was 55-years-old. Daddy was a self-educated, tool and die maker and was never without a job. He read the newspaper, faithfully, and enjoyed word puzzles. Daddy would shame my brothers and me by adding three digit numbers without using his fingers or any other writing materials. Everyone who knew my daddy said that you could set your watch by his actions. He was never late to work or to any other appointments. My father always gave my brothers and me a weekly allowance growing up, beginning at the age of 5. My first allowance was 25 cents; that was a lot of money to a kindergartner. Back then a pack of Now & Later candy was only 5 cents a pack. My brothers and I thought we were rich.

My father was a strict, stern disciplinarian. People that did not know my father thought that he was harsh and unapproachable. He wore a frown that had been etched by the hardships that he had endured. But to those who looked closer, they could see that those lines in my daddy's face told a story of triumph. My daddy told me stories of when Blacks and Whites had separate water fountains, and Blacks were not allowed in most public businesses such as hotels and restaurants, including Detroit's Tiger Baseball Stadium. My father repeatedly taught my brothers and me two important principles to live by throughout our lives. He stated, "A person is the sum total of his or her word, and your word is your bond. Never lie. Never steal. When you die the only thing people will remember about you are your words. Your words represent who you are and what you stand for. When people can no longer believe what comes out of your mouth, you are nothing."

The second principle that daddy hammered in our heads is that we are as good as anybody else. He told us that no matter what anyone tells us, God made us all equal. "The only difference between White and Black people," my daddy said, "is that White people are born with a fair chance to do and be what they want in America. Discipline and hard-work is not enough to make it in this world, make sure that you always fight to have a fair chance like anybody else."

As my daddy lay sleeping in the hospital bed, hooked up to several heart monitors and other medical equipment, I studied his body. I noticed that our hands and feet were identical. My skin color, hairline, legs, nose, hair texture and even blood type are the same as my daddy's. I have been told that I laugh from the gut, loud and hardy just like my daddy. My father molded my determination, ambition and drive, not because we agreed on every issue, but because I was taught to think and be my own person.

When daddy woke up that day, I told him that I loved him and knew that he was tired. "Daddy, I will be okay," I said, "because you gave me strong roots, everything I need to be successful in life." I told my daddy that he was the best father in the world, and that I felt so special and blessed that God would give me such an extraordinary father. I never once asked God to let my father live. I prayed for strength and courage. Upon waking each morning, I thanked Him for the breath in my father's body. The day of my daddy's funeral, I thanked God for the beautiful snowfall that graced the tree branches on the way to the ceme-tery. As I write this I am crying, not because of the loss of my father, but because of the deep appreciation of what I have gained, and the intense joy that I feel for being his daughter. The only true loss would have been to not have such a remarkable father.

Just as I am

♦

The swan gracefully floated down the pond before a strange male duck approached her. "Your neck is long and beautiful," the duck commented, "it gives you an elegant arch on your back that is mesmerizing." The swan began to scrunch her neck down and back as if she was ashamed and stated, "Oh, I have been trying to make my neck much shorter, but I take after my parents. I am really working on improving myself. Do you know of a good neck surgeon?" She then swam away as quickly as she could.

A lion was prowling in the jungle and an elephant stood in awe of his magnificent mane of hair on his face. "Mr. Lion," the elephant said, "your mane gives you a look of power, dignity and respect." The lion was taken by the elephant's compliment and instead of roaring like a lion he purred like a pussy cat stating, "I have been looking for a good barber to cut this old thing off You know, it scares most of the other animals away." The elephant looked at him disappointedly and said, "Oh, I am sorry. I expected you to roar with confidence, I thought you were somebody special."

A small child played and danced in the field with a butterfly and asked it why it didn't fly as high near the sky as the birds. And the butterfly said, "Because then you couldn't see the beautiful, delicate details that God painted on my wings." I thought of this analysis about my own self-esteem as I recently sat in the park observing its beauty. I wondered if the other creatures that God has created apologize for, refute and minimize their uniqueness and gifts. I wondered if other creatures complained to God about hating their lives and wishing they were something different or somewhere else in the world.

I have difficulty accepting compliments. Whenever someone admires my clothes I find it necessary to tell them that I bought it on sale or that I couldn't afford it. "This oh thing, you've gotta be kidding," I would say. If someone praises my hair I assure them that if they were to see me on the weekends they would not think that my hair was so nice. When I was a young child I would dirty my gym shoes before going to school because I didn't want the other children to think they were new. Whenever someone congratulates me on my academic achievements, I will always inform them of my G.E.D out of high school and the tough time I had completing graduate school. If someone appreciates my shape, I let them know that I use to be much smaller.

The compliment that I absolutely have the most problems with is when someone calls me beautiful. After some soul searching I think I understand why I am so insecure about my appearance. It's simple-I didn't create myself I didn't choose my eyes, nose, shape or skin color. If I didn't create myself how can I take credit for it, how can I control it? If I fail a class I can re-take it and study harder the next time. I can re-write an article or change into a more appealing outfit. I can change the color of my lipstick, but the shape of my lips I cannot change. I can enhance and take care of what God has given me, but I can't take credit for the essence of what I am. But most importantly, I have always felt that I could have done a much better job creating myself.

I lost my first beauty contest when I was eight-years-old, to my light complexioned first cousin and my 32 inch walking doll with patches of hair missing from her scalp. The seven and eight-year-old old judges said that I was the darkest of the three therefore I couldn't win. Being taunted as a child for my dark complexion caused me to be angry with God. If I had created myself my lips would have been much smaller, my skin much lighter and my ankles much thinner. I would have been much shorter and small-boned so that I could be a ballerina. I have always questioned, begged and pleaded with the universe to make me a different person. Now I wonder what my life would be like today if I had just graciously accepted myself, instead of pointing out to God all of the characteristics I wished I had possessed.

How can I accept the compliments of others when I have not graciously accepted myself as I am? Who am I to question the magnificent mind of the Universe? God conceived me with the same precision, beauty and judgment that He used when He created the swan, the lion and the butterfly. The only difference is, they are wise enough to know that they are perfect just the way they are. I am working on learning how to just say thank you without feeling guilty or feeling the need to negate the person's compliment. But first I had to start with truly accepting and appreciating myself and then thanking God.

In Barbara Streisand's autobiography she said that people frequently told her that if she wanted to be successful she needed to have a nose job. She said that whenever someone would say this to her she would tell them, "If it's good enough for God, it's good enough for me.

The Other Woman was I

———————— ◆ ————————

I believed him: when he said that his wife no longer loved him; when he said that he was filing for a divorce; and when he said that he had never loved another woman like me. I simply believed him. I never questioned the time that he did not spend with me. I never wondered if he truly loved me. I never doubted the paltry complaints that he made about his wife or if he had ever stopped loving her. Not even once was I concerned about his marriage with her…that is until she called me.

The phone rang. "Hello," I said, but there was nothing but moments of silence. Hesitantly, she asked to speak to me. The sound of her voice lingered in the air and I intuitively knew that it was her, his wife. I could feel our hearts beating as one connected to the same line of drama. I sensed her feelings of agony, sadness and betrayal as we both gently hung up the phone. A deep, nagging pang settled in my abdomen and I was paralyzed in the moment. She reminded me of myself during a period of my life that I never wanted to remember. But I had too soon forgotten what it was like to be on the other side of the phone.

When I was married, my husband told me that there was no one else, but I could sense her between us. I couldn't prove it. I had never even seen traces of her. There were no clichés of lipstick on his collar, hotel receipts or strange phone numbers in his wallet. No, he did not stay out late at night; in fact his actions were very predictable. There was absolutely no tangible evidence, but I knew I had lost him long before he had the courage to leave. Because whomever she was, she had managed to touch my baby so deeply, that only my heart could detect her presence. He denied that she existed and branded me as insecure. How could I ask him to leave a woman who only existed in my imagination?

My imagination was quite vivid. When I snuggled up next to him at night there was no one there. Just the corpse of a man who use to love me. He was obligated to me, but I felt his loyalty to her. I could hear him promising her that he only slept with me, because he had to. I wondered who she was. My mind audited every old girlfriend, coworker and neighbor whom I thought he might be interested in. I wanted to know what she looked like. Were her breasts bigger, smaller, and firmer than mine? Was she prettier than me? I wondered how many times had he made love to her and where and when had he met her. I imagined him caressing her perfect body and declaring his love to her. I tortured myself to sleep each night as his listless body laid next to mine. We both were thinking about her.

I didn't have to search for her phone number because it was always available waiting for me to address, accept and dial reality. I wanted to see why he loved her. So I called her house just to hear her voice. She sounded, so innocent and sweet that it made my heart ache. She thought I was playing on her phone, but I needed to know if she was real. I needed to hear her voice to validate my instincts. No matter how much it hurt, I needed to prove to my husband what my heart had already known. She knew it was me, the other woman because both of our hearts were connected to the same man. I could hear the echo of her thoughts as we both silently, politely hung up the phone. Upon confronting him, the pain and humiliation was unbearable when he said that he needed time because he loved her too. I never asked the other woman to come into my life therefore; I had no right or power to ask her to leave.

I was disgusted with myself for inflicting such horrendous pain on another human being. I had absolutely no excuse because I knew exactly what my lover's wife was going through because I have been on both ends of the phone. And now I was the other woman. I wanted to call her back and tell her that I was so sorry. But I couldn't, because at that point, I loved him too. I demanded that he choose between us. But he clearly stated that there were no easy solutions because he loved both of us and needed time and space to sort his feelings. After a few days of thinking, I decided to treat his wife as if she were me. I asked myself what would I have wanted if I was her. I searched my soul and went back to the exact moment when I suffered the most and my decision was easy, clear and faultless. I told him that I sensed that his wife loved him more than he could ever imagine and I gave him back to her.

My Children Make me a Better Adult

$\blacklozenge$

There is absolutely nothing in my life that 1 am more proud of than my children. Period. This morning I couldn't stop thinking about how much I love them and how my life would be empty and meaningless without their unconditional love. I would give back everything I own, and repeat the most horrendous experiences in my life without a second thought, if God said I had to in order to have my children in my life. In my efforts to raise them with dignity and pride I am challenged to practice the many lessons that I want them to learn. My children complete my being and I am able to see and address my flaws more clearly. My love for them has transformed my life in so many ways.

Their unyielding faith has shown me that in raising them, I must also be prepared to raise myself to heights of character that I thought I was not capable of reaching. I don't know if I can attain the status they have given me, but I do know that my love for them has no bounds and it's endless and timeless. I see the best and worst of myself in my children. When I complain to them about leaving their shoes in the middle of the floor, they always point out to me that I have three pair in the floor-that have been there much longer. I didn't have an answer so now I just make sure that all my things are in place before I chastise them about cleaning their surroundings.

I called my local grocery store livid because many of the items that I had purchased were not there. My nine-year-old son assured me that he had gotten all of the bags out of the trunk because he was looking for his candy. He heard me tell the store clerk that I was disappointed and angry because I was tired and didn't feel like driving back. Something told me to go behind my son and check the car, and sure enough hidden under some things in the trunk were the missing items. I called the grocery store back and apologized for everything I had said. My son made an honest mistake but I should have thoroughly checked the car before calling the store complaining. My son heard me apologize and he asked me to tell them that he was also sorry. The most important thing my son and I learned is that eating crow is not so bad when you sprinkle a little sugar on it.

I tell my children not to answer the door or phone because Mommy doesn't want to be bothered by sales people. On one occasion as we pretended that we were not at home until the knocking on the door ceased, my daughter sat in my lap and whispered in my ear, "Mommy why can't you just tell them the truth?" I was dumbfounded. Gulp! Now that's a concept. I couldn't tell her that I am a wimp and many times I don't know how to be firm and tell people, "No, I am not interested."

I can't count how many times I have switched long distance carriers and bought more Girl Scout cookies than could be eaten in one year. My daughter's innocent words haunted me that night and I decided that this is not the type of character or courage that I want her to display when some boy pressures her for sex before she's ready or her peers try to entice her to use illegal drugs. So now, I suck in my gut and answer the door, because I know my babies are watching my every move.

I find that I am much more effective with my children when I direct my children's behaviors by my own actions. I am no saint and this is not an easy feat for me. However when I see the characteristics in my children that I admire about myself it encourages me to work much harder at being a better person. My son is now competing with me to see who can read the most books in the shortest period of time. If I continue using profanity at this pace my daughter will be a millionaire before she is twenty. I have agreed to give her a dollar for each curse word used in her presence. I love classical music because it inspires me. When I listen to music I would have my children describe what they see in their imagination. Now my son asks me, "Mommy, what do you see in this music? I see a horse galloping in the rain."

I don't know which goal takes precedence over the other; me wanting to be someone that my children can be proud or helping them to develop themselves into people that they themselves can respect and admire. The two are so interrelated that no matter which way I go the results may be the same. For me being a parent is not just about wanting to give love, but being open and vulnerable enough to receive it; it's not having all the answers but being big enough to say "I don't know let's find out together; and it's not about theoretically being right because I am the grown up, but doing the right thing even when I am embarrassed and know that I am wrong. The purity and intensity of my children's love continues to chisel me into a statue of integrity that I can be proud of. But I will be the first to admit that their work is cut out for them.

If I am so Beautiful, Why am I Alone?

◆

"What fool could have possibly divorced you," the store clerk asked during a general conversation. I know that people are complimenting me, but when I hear comments like these I feel awful. If I am so beautiful and intelligent why did my ex-husband go months and months with out having sex with me? Is there some kind of contradiction here? When men would come on to me, deep down inside I would think to myself, once you get to know me you won't think I am so wonderful. It really did not matter to me that other men found me attractive when the man who I thought loved me would not touch me without begging him for sex.

Many of my female co-workers and friends have experienced the same dilemma. One friend said that she had over twenty thousand dollars worth of cosmetic surgery performed on her body pending her divorce. One of my associates stated that she went on a "tramping-spree." She stated that she slept with three men in one night after breaking up with her boyfriend. "I felt so unattractive. After going together for four years he would not sleep in the same bed with me and washed up immediately following sex. I never felt beautiful enough or clean enough," she said. "It's really weird," said Barbara, the thought of sex with my husband made me sick to the stomach, but I felt that he should at least come on to me. He's a man and men are suppose to want sex no matter what. Since he was not acting the male part, it must be because some important piece of femininity was missing from me."

I asked a few male friends if they had ever been in a relationship with a woman and had gone without sex for long periods and if so why. "Its not that you don't still find the woman physically appealing all the time, it's just that the lines of communication have broken down so much, that it's what's inside that turns a lot of men off," Jay replied. Bill interrupted, "I know sometimes I'll think to myself when I get home I am going to work on my marriage or I'll think about parts of her body that arouses me, but the minute I walk in the door she starts about the bills, the garbage needs taking out, the kids, etc. My thoughts of sexual arousal are diminished because she reminds me of a nag or worse yet, my mother." Rick explained, "Some men claim that it's the woman's weight that turns them off sexually, but I don't think it's true for most men. I agree with the other guys, it is usually so much resentment built up in the relationship, that it is difficult to feel sexual arousal and anger at the same time."

The American society socializes women to associate their self worth with their sexual desirability. The media constantly reminds us to increase or decrease our breasts, buttocks, thighs, lips, hair etc. On the other hand, men are socialized to appreciate mainly the physical attributes of females as a characteristic of being masculine. "Are you a breasts man or leg man," they ask each other? Society's expectations of male and female roles sometimes steer both sexes away from matters of the human heart. Most marriage counselors agree that sex is the gauge that measures the health of marriages and relationships. It is difficult for couples to correct problems in the relationship, when neither party can agree on what the real issues are that need to be addressed.

In my previous relationship I would check the scale, my hair, make-up, breasts size, every thing but my attitude when there was a problem in my relationship. Not when the problems were obvious, but when I just sensed something wasn't right. I now know it wasn't my perfume.

In my new relationship I check what's going on with my man. I want to know what he's thinking and feeling when things are not right between us. To my surprise, most of the time it is not something I did or did not do. He might have had a bad day at work and wants to be left alone or various minor problems that fade in the morning without a thousand questions from me assuming that I am the center of most of his problems. Sometimes the best way to help is by just being in the next room.

I now understand the difference between the sexual attractiveness that keep a man and the kind that make men notice me on the streets. Men on the street make catcalls because it is a part of their male behavior. Maybe he liked the way my ass fit in my jeans, or my legs or outfit; but the truth of the matter is, it doesn't mean anything to him. Therefore, why should I base any part of my self-esteem on this superficial mating ritual of the male human species? It is just a regular part of his day as a male. The kind of attractiveness that men want to make love to over and over again, is being emotionally attentive, listening to his concerns after a stressful day and most important of all is making him feel like he matters even if he did not have a penis.

Before I Let Him In

$\blacklozenge$

"You know, the problem with women," he argued, "is that they have too many sexual hang ups that reduces their ability to enjoy sex. If a woman is attracted to a man and wants to f—k him, she can't because she is worried about being labeled a tramp, promiscuous or a whore. I know that women have the same physical sexual needs as men, and I don't feel like I should have to wine and dine her when she wants it as bad as I do.

I think my male friend may be correct in his assessment of how society has socialized women to suppress their sexual feelings or use sex for barter and trade. Maybe women should open up more and share their bodies indiscriminately and let passion free them from social oppression. However, intercourse is not merely a physical act for me, when I let a man enter my body, he must first develop a relationship with my soul. I don't care what others think about my sexual behavior, just the trusting eyes of the woman who stares back at me each morning in the mirror. She is the part of me who demands that the intruder loves, respects and accepts all of who I am.

There are some things that a man must know about me before I can let him in. First, if he is only seeking gratification in the most superficial sense, I must warn him that where he wants to enter he won't find me there. Any woman could substitute the pleasure he seeks from my body, if he would but only close his eyes. There's nothing unique about the sex act itself, women come in different shapes and sizes and any honest man will tell you that it's all the same. What really makes sex extraordinary is the respect and emotional attachment between a man and a woman. And I don't think one date is enough time for a man to learn how delicious and special I really am.

If a man really wants to enjoy being with me sexually there are three main things that he must know: where I have been; where I am going; and what he needs to do when he gets there. Did you know that I am very sensitive and when you say you will call, I will patiently wait by the phone? I have been hurt so many times in the past, and though I play strong and tough, my heart is fragile. So please don't say you will call, if you really don't mean it. Even if you don't call as you promised, the next time I hear from you, I will pretend that it didn't matter. Just be assured that I won't find you worthy to come in.

Be my friend. Show me that I can trust you. Look beyond my eyes and tell me what you see. Do you think I am smart? Did you know that I have a dark sense of humor and many times I laugh to keep from crying? The first time you see me without my phony make-up mask that I present to the public, you'll know that you're getting closer to my heart and to discovering and understanding who I really am, so tell me that I am beautiful anyway. I am an educated, financially independent woman and I plan to travel the world. I can buy my own dinner, clothes, car and pay my own rent, but if all you can offer is what I turn down from other men all day long, keep moving. I need you to love me before I can let you in.

Please tell me more about you, what type of relationship are you looking for? Do you plan to marry someday? Do you have or want children? Have you practiced safe sex? Have you ever hit a woman? What qualities do you look for in a woman outside of bed and do I meet any them? What was your childhood like-and by the way, what is your middle name? Let's establish some boundaries and rules so that neither one of us will get hurt. Eventually, if our relationship progresses, I would like to know what pleases you sexually, I am quite sure that you are not like any other man I have dated and I need some time to learn how to treat you like the special man that I know you are.

My boyfriend tells me that he is faithful to me because he loves me, but accuses me of only being faithful to him because of my own personal philosophy about fidelity as opposed to having a deep abiding love for him. He is right, I am faithful to me. I love him, but if we were to separate, I would not be looking to sexually abandon myself to the first strange man that I am attracted to. My boyfriend did his homework and he knew what to do when he got there, so there is no need for him to worry about intruders. I am a serial, monogamous kind-of-girl, and when I let a man in, I plan on keeping him around for a long time.

The Duality of Sexuality

———————— ◆ ————————

What is it about the luminous energy force that creates all human life that also has the power to destroy the soul of its hapless victims? President Clinton and Monica Lewinsky; Gary Hart and Donna Rice; Clarence Thomas and Anita Hill; Mike Tyson and What's Her Name know all too well, that if you want to destroy a man, don't trap him in tax fraud, murder or stealing money from the poor. If you truly want to bring a man down-find a woman. Not an army, FBI, CIA, or any brute strength or intricate level of plotting and planning, but the essence of its exact opposite…simplicity, beauty, innocence, softness, a furtive grin, a sweet hello. This all-encompassing energy that is the foundation of families, builder of dreams, seller of any and everything that one can imagine from cars to magazines has the innate ability to perish all that it creates.

Vanessa L. Williams's sexual magnetism was responsible for her winning and losing her crown as Ms. America. The sexual exclusiveness in a committed relationship bonds the couple; however, when this sacred passion is inadvertently shared outside of its realm the contents are diminished. Sex sells magazines, clothes, and toothpaste. Women have been fired from jobs for posing in nude magazines, wearing too short dresses and not wearing bras. Stars have been carved from the precious stones of pure sex appeal such as Marilyn Monroe, Playboy Magazine's first nude model. Businesses have been boycotted because of carrying sexually explicit items. Sex is sacred, yet mundane, electrifying, but stultifying, beautiful, and vulgar. The ambiguity and hypocrisy surrounding this three-letter-word has existed since Adam and Eve.

Why is sex so powerful? Not only sex, but all of the rudimentary elements in life are the most powerful and potent sources in the universe. Water is beautiful and mesmerizing. Go view the oceans, seas, lakes and rivers. Observe their rainbow of beautiful colors; look at the waves and ripples. Study their beauty and feel their power. Water is needed to sustain all forms of life. It provides an atmosphere that connects and separates worlds, cultures, nations, and ethnic groups. This same entity is used to grow a garden, bathe a baby and make lemonade. Feel its diversity when kissing in the rain, taking a warm bubble bath and drinking a cold glass of water. Water has the power to sink a ship; rainstorms destroy cities towns and villages. People choke while drinking water and millions of people have drowned while swimming, surfing, and boating.

Fire has the same qualities. A fireplace in a home can be very beautiful and romantic. Listen to its soothing sound, the soft crackling of wood. Watch the array of colors in a campfire-the pretty blues, and shades of red, orange and gold. Feel the warmth that illuminates from its heat while cuddled up to someone you love or sitting in a circle with friends telling stories. Have you ever watched a flickering candle? The beauty of a candlelit room is unmatched in a church while the choir softly sings Christmas carols or when making love with someone special. Smell the aroma of momma's fried chicken, food cooked on a grill or toasted marshmallows. Fire can light a cigarette and burn down a home. It has destroyed forests, villages, cars and people.

The things that make life wonderful many times are the same things that can make life exceedingly miserable. The duality and opposition of its nature is the essence and strength of its greatness. There is one significant difference when comparing sex, water, and fire. Most of the time societies can control its views, feelings and behaviors that renders power to human sexuality. Water and fire is neither good nor bad. When someone is killed in a fire or rainstorm we do not view its source as evil or bad. We handle these forces with care because we respect its weaknesses and strengths. Human sexuality is the most potent force in human relations. None of us would be alive today if this energy was not brought to fruition.

Sex scandals are the oldest tricks in the book, the incipient victims were Adam and Eve and Samson and Delilah. They surface right before critical speeches, elections, wars, and job promotions. The contents do not enlighten, enhance or improve the general public's awareness, policies or laws. Society's obsession with sex scandals is not merely an issue of morality, but our own dual dispositions regarding sex. Sex scandals reflect the detestation that we have with our selves for finding someone else attractive out side of our committed relationship, admiring someone of the same sex or being sexually aroused by our mate's friend. The sex scandal allows us to feel good about ourselves for resisting what we perceive as loathsome, immoral feelings that we have been able to suppress and avoid.

Whether or not the accusations are true or false is not nearly as important as humankind's inability to understand and embrace its sexuality as something beautiful, yet powerful; and should be handled with respect and care.